Windows
Internet Security:
The Essential Guide

Published by Agora Business Publications LLP

Agora Business Publications LLP
Nesfield House
Broughton Hall Business Park
Skipton
BD23 3AN

Publisher: Victoria Burrill
Author: Stefan Johnson

Phone: 01756 693 180
Fax: 01756 693 196
Email: cs@agorapublications.co.uk
Web: www.agorabusinesspublications.co.uk

ISBN: 978-1-908245-06-9

Agora Business Publications LLP. Nesfield House, Broughton Hall Business Park, Skipton, Yorkshire, BD23 3AN.
Registered in England No. OC323533, VAT No. GB 893 3184 95.

Table of Contents

Windows Internet Security

Dear Reader,

These days most PCs are permanently connected to the Internet by high-speed broadband, meaning that the probability of danger increases, as hackers and viruses are given more opportunity to gain unauthorised access to your computer. In order to efficiently protect your PC and home networks against online attacks, effective security measures are an absolute must. In this book, you will find the most important protective and preventive measures which you can use to seal off your Windows system from viruses, hackers, Bots and Internet fraud. I'll show you how to:

1. Fight off viruses, worms and Trojans with a virus scanner.

2. Use a firewall to protect your PC against Internet attacks.

3. Safely and effectively fight Spam and advertising emails.

4. Avoid the threat of data-stealing spyware.

5. Safeguard yourself 100% against Internet fraud.

6. Protect your Windows system against hidden rootkits.

7. Tweak hidden registry settings to boost the security of Internet Explorer.

Best regards,

Stefan Johnson

1: Protect Yourself Against Viruses, Worms and Trojans

There are many errors and serious system crashes that can crop up on a Windows PC, but there are few more serious than your PC getting infected with a virus. Initially you probably won't even know that you are infected, but as your PC starts to behave more and more erratically, as the virus downloads and installs new infections from the Internet and systematically destroys the important files on your PC, you'll soon see the tell-tale signs, such as a sluggish PC or random windows popping up without any explanation.

The Types of Virus that Can Strike Your PC

The term malware is used to describe the many different types of malicious software that can attack your PC, either to render it unusable, to target you with unwanted advertising, or to steal sensitive data from your hard drive. Some malware will run silently in the background on your PC, but the vast majority will cause your PC to misbehave, making it very apparent that your PC is infected. Different types of malware have different tell-tale signs of infection.

Below we explain the differences between some of the most common types of malware you are likely to come across, and the signs of infection that you should look out for.

How to Spot a Virus/Worm Infection

Originally, a virus would spread itself by copying its code into the code of another application, so that when the host application was executed the virus code would also be run – the name virus is gained by analogy with a biological virus which spreads by copying itself into the DNA of a host organism. Typically, the virus code will delete important files or otherwise disrupt the system. Nowadays, viruses also spread themselves through other means, such as by infecting Word documents and allocations that use macro or scripting languages such as VBA (Visual Basic for Applications).

There are several common subtypes of virus that might infect your computer. Some of the most common are:

- **Macro virus** – a Macro virus is often written in a scripting language such as Visual Basic Script (VBS) and is designed to infect programs that include script execution facilities such as Word and Excel. These viruses will be run inside the target application, and are very often designed to cause corruption in documents that you are editing and spread by copying themselves to new documents that you create in the targeted application.

- **Network virus** – this type of virus is designed to spread itself via a local area network or even the Internet, usually via a shared file system. Once a machine is infected, the virus will scan its shared network drives looking for further opportunities to spread itself.

- **Logic bomb** – a logic bomb is designed to stay inert until certain specific conditions are met, and then performs some action such as displaying a message or deleting files. One common condition looked for by logic bombs is the arrival of a certain date (such as Friday the 13th) which will then cause it to become active.

Worms are designed to crawl through a network from computer to computer spreading their infection. Once they have infected one machine they use its network connection to scan for other machines vulnerable to infection. This can be via email or by exploiting vulnerabilities in the operating system or software running on a PC.

Usually a worm will be designed to do something more malicious than just copying itself from machine to machine. For example, it could be used to spread a program that deleted files from your system, or provide a backdoor for hackers to access your machine. The key difference between a virus and a worm is that a worm can propagate itself, whereas a virus requires some kind of host, usually a worm or infected application to transmit it.

Signs of a virus/worm infection

- Strange error or warning messages being displayed on your screen, particularly if they purport to come from a virus.

- Strange sounds, music or speech playing through your PC's speakers that is not obviously connected to a running application.

- You find that a large amount of your system's memory is taken up when you open the Task Manager (by pressing [**Ctrl**] + [**Alt**] + [**Del**] and clicking on the **Task Manager** option if prompted).

- The name of your hard drive has been changed in Computer (My Computer in XP).

- Your application programs have been removed, files have been deleted from your hard drive or have become corrupt.

- Software has been installed on your system mysteriously.

Tell-tale Signs of a Trojan Infection

Like the Trojan horse of Greek mythology, a Trojan is a piece of malicious software designed to look like some innocent application. The idea is that the user will be tricked into running the application (very often on a website that warns you that your computer is at risk) and then install some other infection on their system. The difference between a Trojan and a virus is that a Trojan does not replicate itself, instead it relies on user actions to spread.

Signs of Trojan infection

- The picture on your monitor is corrupt, rotated or otherwise mangled.

- Your desktop wallpaper, background colour or window colours change by themselves.

- Documents or messages print on your printer by themselves.

- The screen saver settings change by themselves.

- Your mouse is not working correctly, for example, the right and left mouse buttons reverse their functions, or your mouse pointer disappears or moves by itself.

- Your Windows Start button or taskbar disappears.

- Your computer shuts down and powers off by itself.

Harness Windows Security Features to Protect Your PC

As the security threats facing Windows have increased with the growth of the Internet, Microsoft have developed new built-in features designed to help combat the threat. These features go some way to combating some of the threats that can affect your PC, but as you will see later in this chapter, they can't beat the power of a third party virus checker for keeping you protected. In the table below, we summarise some of the most useful security features built into Windows:

Feature	Description	Windows Versions
Action Center/ Security Center	Introduced with Windows XP Service Pack 2, the Security Center provides a single control panel from which to control your Windows Updates, anti-virus software and firewall. Security Center provides a service to monitor the status of third party anti-virus software and alert you if it is out-of-date. In Windows 7, the Security Center has been renamed the Action Center, and covers both Windows security and maintenance.	Windows 7/Vista/XP SP2
Windows Firewall	A firewall has been present since Windows 2000, but only came to prominence with the release of XP Service Pack 2. The firewall protects your PC by blocking external software connecting to your machine across the Internet. A firewall is essential to protect against hackers trying to exploit security flaws in Windows software to gain access to your machine.	Windows 7/Vista/ XP
Windows Defender	Windows Defender, formerly known as Windows AntiSpyware, is a spyware protection and removal tool. It is installed by default on Windows 7 and Vista systems, and available as a separate download for Windows XP. You can download it from: http://tiny.cc/59g14.	Windows 7/Vista/XP

Feature	Description	Windows Versions
Data Execution Prevention	Data Execution Prevention (DEP) is a system designed to protect against bugs in software that can be exploited by hackers to gain access to your PC. Two types of DEP exist, one based solely in software, and one which uses advanced features of modern CPUs to provide enhanced protection.	Windows 7/Vista/XP SP2
Address Space Layout Randomization	Address Space Layout Randomization is a security technique that protects your PC by randomly arranging key pieces of data in the system memory in order to make it more difficult for hackers and virus writers to exploit faults in the system software.	Windows 7/Vista
User Account Control	If you're a Windows Vista user you're bound to have come across User Account Control (UAC). It is the component responsible for throwing up warning messages every time you try to make the smallest change to your system's settings. The theory behind UAC is that a malicious program couldn't attack your PC without being explicitly authorised by the user, although UAC has proved so annoying in Vista that most users turn it off. Microsoft have addressed some of the criticisms in Windows 7 by making UAC much more configurable.	Windows 7/Vista

Access the Action Center via **Start** > **Control Panel** > **Action Center** (**Security Center** in Windows Vista/XP). From here you can monitor your anti-virus software, firewall and Windows Update status.

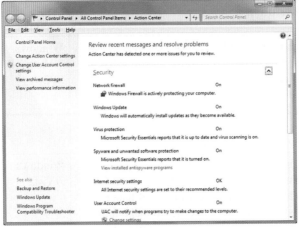

Control security settings from the Action Center

Windows has many features that can help secure your PC against infection by malicious software, but they are no use if not properly configured. To make sure that your PC is as well protected as possible, you should spend a few minutes applying the quick tips in the rest of this chapter.

Enable Windows Update to Minimise Security Bugs

Automatically updating Windows with the latest fixes from Microsoft will help protect against one of the most common attack methods (or 'vectors' in security parlance) – faulty Windows components. If you don't already have Automatic Updates enabled, you can switch it on as follows:

1. Click **Start > Control Panel > Windows Update** (**Automatic Updates** in XP). Click **Change Settings** in Windows 7/Vista.

2. Select **Automatic** or **Install updates automatically (recommended)** ① and set the time you would like Windows to check for updates each day ②.

3. Click **OK** to finish.

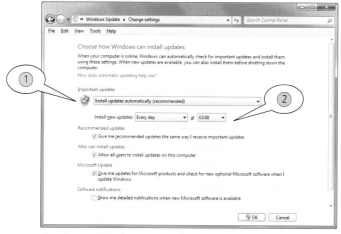

Configure Windows to update automatically

If you haven't previously had Automatic Updates enabled, you should manually update your system as follows, to ensure the latest software fixes are installed:

Windows 7/Vista

1. Click **Start > All Programs > Windows Update**.

2. Follow the prompts to install updates on your system.

Windows XP

3. Click **Start > All Programs > Internet Explorer**.

4. Click **Tools > Windows Update** (or **Safety > Windows Update** in depending on the version of IE you have). If prompted, choose to run the ActiveX control.

5. Click **Express** to check for new updates.

6. If any updates are found, choose to install them.

Prevent Macro Viruses from Hiding in Word Documents

Although less common than they used to be, viruses transmitted through infected Word documents are still a threat to Windows users. They exploit the ability of Word documents to carry program code, called Macros, which were originally intended by Microsoft to make documents more interactive. They can easily be prevented by disabling the Macro feature of Word as follows:

Word 2010/2007

1. Click on the **File** (**Office** in Word 2007) button in the top left-hand corner then click **Options** (Word Options in 2007).

2. Click **Trust Center > Trust Center Settings**.

3. Select **Disable all macros without notification** ③ then click **OK > OK**.

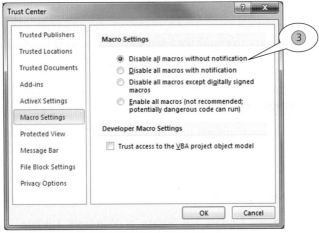

Disable macro viruses in Microsoft Word

Word 2003/2002/2000

1. Click **Tools > Macro > Security**.

2. Click on the **Security Level** tab then click **Very High** (**High** in Word 2000).

3. Click **OK** to finish.

Enable Data Execution Prevention to Block Insecure Applications

The Data Execution Prevention feature that first shipped with Windows XP SP2 should be enabled by default. You can check, and enable it if necessary, as follows:

1. Click **Start** > **Control Panel** > **System**. Click **Advanced system settings** in Windows 7/Vista.

2. Click **Advanced**, then **Settings** under the **Performance** heading.

3. Click the **Data Execution Prevention** tab.

4. Select **Turn on DEP for all programs and services except those I select**.

5. Click **OK**.

If you find you are having problems with an application after enabling DEP, you can add that application as an exception as follows:

1. Open the DEP window by following steps 1–3 above.

2. Click **Add**, browse for the **.EXE** file of the application that you want to add an exception for (which will probably be stored in the **C:\Program Files** folder), then click **Open**.

3. Click **OK**.

Check for Suspicious Network Activity

A tell-tale sign of malware infection is increased Internet traffic, as the infection tries to 'phone home' to its creator, and potentially download new infections to your machine. If your system is behaving erratically and you suspect you have some kind of infection, you can check up on the applications using your network connection as follows:

1. Click **Start** > **All Programs** > **Accessories** right-click on **Command Prompt** and choose **Run as administrator** (XP users just click **Command Prompt**).

2. At the command prompt, type **NETSTAT -a -b** and press [**Enter**].

3. A list of application that are using your Internet connection will be displayed ④.

Check for suspicious activity with NETSTAT

TIP! If you don't recognise any of the applications displayed in the list, search for them on the website www.processlibrary.com. This site will tell you whether the application is harmless, or whether it is a malware infection.

Boost UAC Security in Windows 7

Unlike Vista, Windows 7 gives you much more fine grained control over which UAC messages are displayed. However, for the best protection, you should configure the highest level of UAC possible, by following the steps below:

1. Click **Start > Control Panel > User Accounts**.

2. Click **Change User Account Control settings**.

3. Set the slider to the top most position ⑤ and click **OK** ⑥.

Using UAC requires you to balance security with usability. If you find that the highest level of UAC protection is too intrusive, try turning it down one notch on the slider. You will see less warning messages, but your PC will also be less secure.

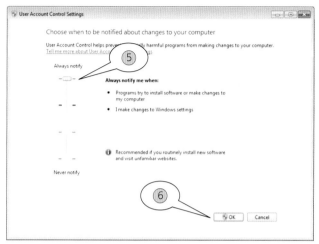

Configure UAC security in Windows 7

Use Windows Defender to Remove Infections from Your System

Windows Defender is available for Windows 7, Vista and XP, and can be downloaded from: http://tiny.cc/59g14 (it should be installed by default if you have Windows 7 or Vista). Once installed, it will monitor your system for any incoming malware infections, and periodically scan your machine for infections.

Before the first time you use Windows Defender, configure it to remove all of the threats that it detects, however serious, as follows:

1. Click **Start > All Programs > Windows Defender**.

2. Click **Tools > Options**.

3. Under the **Default actions** heading, set all of the drop-down lists to **Remove** ⑦.

4. Click **Save**.

11

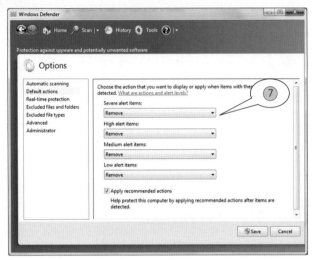

Configure Windows Defender to remove all threats

Once Windows Defender is configured, you can scan your system for malicious software at any time as follows:

1. Click **Start** > **All Programs** > **Windows Defender**.

2. Click the drop-down arrow next to **Scan** and choose **Full Scan**.

3. The full scan of your system will take some time to complete. Once it does, remove any infections if prompted.

4 Essential Steps to Remove Any Virus from Your PC

If a virus or other malware program does manage to get itself installed on your system, it may well disable your current anti-virus software (if you have any) to prevent you from removing it from your PC. If this happens then you will need to boot your system in Safe Mode and then scan your system with your virus checker. Follow the four steps below to clean your system.

Step 1: Turn off System Restore

Many viruses conceal themselves on your system by hiding in System Restore points, which often virus checkers don't or can't scan. For this reason, you should temporarily turn off System Restore until you have removed the infections on your PC. To turn off System Restore, follow the steps below:

Windows 7

1. Click **Start > Control Panel > System**.

2. Click **Advanced system settings > System Protection**.

3. Click **Configure > Turn off system protection** ⑧.

4. Click **OK** ⑨ **> OK**.

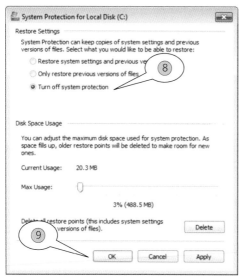

Control System Restore in Windows 7

Windows Vista

1. Click **Start > Control Panel > System**.

2. Click **Advanced system settings > System Protection**.

3. Under **Available Disks**, untick each one of the listed hard drives.

4. Click **OK**.

Windows XP

1. Click **Start > Control Panel > System**.

2. Click **System Restore**, then tick **Turn off System Restore on all drives or Turn off System Restore** depending on the option shown.

3. Click **Apply > OK** to finish.

Once you've completed checking and cleaning your PC, you should turn System Restore back on by repeating the above steps.

Step 2: Boot your system in Safe Mode

In order to ensure that the virus isn't loaded into memory when you perform your virus scan, you should boot your system into Safe Mode as follows:

1. Re-boot your PC and repeatedly press [**F8**] and your PC boots.

2. The Advanced Options menu will be displayed. Use the [**Up Arrow**] and [**Down Arrow**] keys to select **Safe Mode**, then press [**Enter**].

3. Your PC will boot in to safe mode. If prompted, click **Yes** to confirm that you want to work in Safe Mode once Windows loads.

Step 3: Remove Adware and Spyware Infections

Once in Safe Mode, install Malwarebytes Anti-Malware which can be downloaded from: http://tiny.cc/sj4u7. With the software installed, you should give your system a full scan as follows:

1. Click **Start > All Programs > Malwarebytes AntiMalware > Malwarebytes AntiMalware**.

2. Click on the **Scanner** tab ⑩.

3. Select **Perform full scan**, then click **Scan**.

4. Select all of the drives displayed and click **Scan**.

5. If any infections are discovered, choose to remove them.

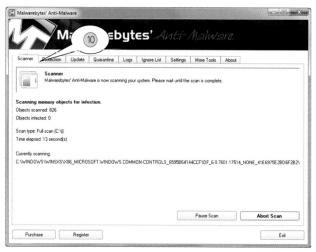

Use Anti-Malware to remove infections from your PC

Step 4: Scan your PC with AVG

After removing any adware or spyware infections from your system, you should install AVG which can be downloaded from: http://tiny.cc/7u3xn. If you have any other anti-virus software installed you will need to remove it using the Programs and Features control panel (Add or Remove Programs in XP) before installing AVG.

If possible, you should update AVG before running a scan, to ensure that AVG knows about all of the latest virus definitions. To do this, you will need to download the latest update from http://free.avg.com/download-update.

Do this on a PC not infected with viruses, and either burn the update file to CD or save it to a USB memory stick. On the infected PC you should now update AVG as follows:

1. Insert the CD or USB drive containing your AVG update in to the infected PC.

2. Click **Start > All Programs > AVG Free > AVG User Interface**.

3. Click **Tools > Update from directory...**

4. Browse to and select the drive containing the update file that you downloaded, then click **OK**.

5. Click **Close** when the update is finished.

Next, you should run as full system scan by following the steps below:

1. Click **Start > All Programs > AVG Free > AVG User Interface**.

2. Click **Update Now** ⑪ to install the latest virus detection routines.

3. Click **Scan now** ⑫.

4. The scan will take some time to complete. Once it is complete, any infections found will be displayed. If prompted, you should choose to remove them.

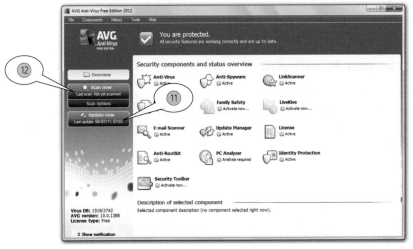

Give your PC a complete system scan

Once AVG has scanned your PC, re-boot Windows into normal mode. You should now be virus-free, but ensure that you perform regular scans with AVG to keep your system clean.

Perform an Essential Security Audit to Test Your Anti-Virus Software

The importance of having security software installed on your computer can never be overstated as there are very real dangers from a variety of online threats such as viruses and other forms of malware. But with so many different categories of security software – firewalls, antivirus, anti-malware, phishing filters, pop-up blockers and more besides – and countless programs to choose from in each category, it can be difficult to decide which to use.

It may be the case that you have installed an old security tool which does not offer protection against the latest threats, or it may not be properly configured meaning that full protection is not provided. Simply installing security tools and trusting that they will function in the way they claim can lure you into a false sense of security – and this can have potentially dangerous consequences. Using old anti-malware software can be as dangerous as having none installed.

Make Sure Your Anti-Virus Software is Actually Working

Nobody wants to purposely install a virus on their computer just to test the anti-virus software that is installed – this is potentially dangerous – but thankfully there are some safe virus test files that can be used instead.

Assuming that virus protection is installed and working, the 'fake' viruses should be detected and this gives a fair indication of whether real viruses will also be picked up:

1. Navigate to the eicar website at http://tiny.cc/i7ohu, click **Download**, then scroll down the page to locate the four file download links.

2. Right-click each link in turn and select the **Save file as** or **Save target as** option and save the files to the desktop.

3. During the download process it is possible that the files will be detected as viruses, in which case you should select the option to move them into quarantine.

4. If the test viruses are not automatically detected, manually run a virus scan using the anti-virus software you have installed to check its effectiveness.

When the checks have been performed, it is likely that you will want to remove the virus test files, even though they are quite safe and will not infect your PC. However, it is possible that an effective virus scanner will block access to the files which may prevent them from being deleted – the only option here is to temporarily disable your anti-virus software, restart Windows and then delete the files. It is important that the disabling of protection is only temporary and that it is re-enabled as soon as the files have been removed.

If the virus test files have not been detected or flagged on your computer, it could be because you do not have anti-virus software installed. Check the settings, or install AVG as described on page 15.

Ensure the Built-in Security Features of Your Browser are Configured Correctly

Most web browsers have a range of security features built into them that help protect against virus infections. As new methods of exploiting problems with web browsers are frequently discovered, it can be difficult to test your vulnerability to all of them. However, there are a few tests which are worth performing to see if you are protected against some of the most common problems:

1. Pay a visit to the following browser security tests website at http://tiny.cc/4b0ii.

2. Click the button labelled **How Does Your Browser Compare**.

3. Click the button **Go to the Security Tests**.

4. Untick the option **Share my results**, then click the button **Run the Security Tests**.

5. The test results will show where your browser security is lacking, and where you are protected.

The best way to ensure that your web browser offers the maximum possible protection is to check that you are using the very latest version – this will mean that all of the most recent bug fixes and patches are installed and that you have access to the most recent security features. Use the steps given earlier in this chapter to ensure that Windows Update is enabled.

Checklist: Ensure You Stay Protected from PC Viruses

✓ Keeping Windows and all of your software applications up-to-date will limit the chances that viruses and other malicious software get to infect your PC.

✓ Running a virus checker will ensure that your PC is on the lookout for virus infections before they are able to get on your system, meaning that the threat can be neutralised before it does any damage.

✓ By regularly testing your anti-virus software using the steps given in this chapter, you will be able to detect potential holes in your security before they lead to infection.

✓ Infections can also enter your PC via contaminated removable drives, such as USB memory sticks and floppy disks. Your anti-virus software should pick up any infections, but be wary of clicking on files contained on removable drives if you aren't sure where they've come from.

✓ Removing infections often requires you to run a range of different software, to ensure that all possible malware programs are removed fully.

✓ Suspicious network activity can be an indication that you have a virus infection, so if your Internet connection seems sluggish, be sure to check your PC.

2: Use a Firewall to Protect Your PC Against Internet Attacks

If you use the Internet, it is absolutely essential that you install and run a firewall, to protect yourself from hacker attacks and virus infection. Each PC and server connected to the Internet has a number of 'virtual ports' which act rather like old telephone switchboards, which other PCs connect to.

Different Internet applications use different default ports. For example, when you use your web browser to visit www.windowsadvisor.co.uk, your web browser connects to port 80 (the default web browsing port) on the server www.windowsadvisor.co.uk and downloads the web page to display on your screen. This is called an outbound connection, since your PC is connecting out to another machine.

Similarly, machines on the Internet can connect to programs running on your PC. This is called an inbound connection, and is potentially more problematic, as hackers and virus writers will often try to exploit weaknesses in software listening out for inbound connections in order to gain unauthorised access to your PC.

A firewall helps prevent these problems by blocking access to ports. It is most useful when blocking access to inbound ports, since it will prevent hackers from trying to force access through open ports. The safest setting is to block access to all inbound ports, however, some applications won't function if the ports they use are blocked, so the trick is to open as few ports as possible, to minimise the risk of infection.

Many firewalls also allow you to block outbound access too, which can be useful when trying to prevent Trojans and other infections that might infiltrate your PC from sending information back to their creators. However, in practice this can be quite restrictive, since many applications (such as your web browser, email client and even Microsoft Word) cannot function if they cannot access the Internet.

Since Windows XP Service Pack 2 (SP2), Windows has had a well featured built-in firewall, but the features of the built-in firewall differ across Windows versions. The table below summarises the key features of the firewall in different Windows versions:

Version	Features
Windows 7	Windows 7 firewall can block both inbound and outbound connections, and has the capability to apply different settings (called profiles) to different types of network at the same time – home and public networks, for example, meaning you can have a different firewall running on your wireless network to your wired network, and operating at the same time.
Windows Vista	Like the Windows 7 firewall, the Vista firewall can also block inbound and outbound connections. The Vista firewall also supports multiple profiles, but only one may be used at a time.
Windows XP SP2	The XP SP2 firewall only blocks inbound Internet connections. If you need to block outbound connections, you will need to install a third party firewall.

In addition to the Windows firewall, if you use a router to connect to the Internet, it will almost certainly have an extra built-in firewall, meaning you are doubly protected.

In this chapter we'll look at how to configure all of your firewalls for ultimate security.

Security Essential: Check the Firewall is Running

By default on Windows XP Service Pack 2 and above, the Windows Firewall should be enabled. However, certain security software and virus infections can disable the Windows Firewall, so it's worth periodically checking that it is still running. To check, follow the steps below:

Windows 7

1. Click **Start > Control Panel**.

2. Click **Action Center**.

3. Expand the **Security** ① section and check that Windows Firewall is listed as being on ②.

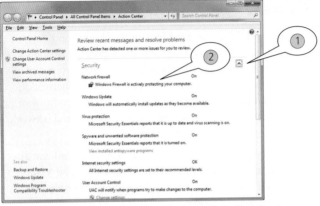

Check the firewall settings in Windows 7 Action Center

Windows Vista/XP

1. Click **Start > Control Panel**.

2. Double-click **Security Centre**.

3. Check that the Firewall setting is **On**. You can expand the Firewall menu to see details.

Quickly Enable the Windows Firewall for Crucial PC Protection

If you find that the firewall is not turned on, then enable it as follows:

Windows 7

1. Click **Start > Control Panel**.

2. Click **Windows Firewall**.

3. Click **Turn Windows Firewall on or off**.

4. Select **Turn Windows Firewall on** for both **Home and Private Networks** and **Public Networks** ③.

5. Click **OK** ④.

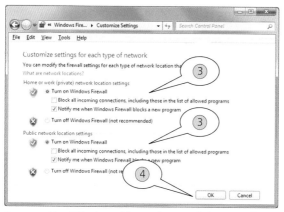

Turn on the Windows Firewall essential protection

Windows Vista

1. Click **Start > Control Panel**.

2. Double-click **Windows Firewall**.

3. Click **Turn Windows Firewall on or off**.

4. Set the Firewall setting to **On (recommended)**.

5. Click **OK**.

Windows XP

1. Open **Start > Control Panel**.

2. Double-click the **Windows Firewall** icon.

3. Click the radio button next to **On (recommended)**.

4. Click **OK**.

Quickly Configure a Firewall Exception to Troubleshoot Application Errors

When an application needs to open a port, often Windows will pop-up a warning message asking you to approve the firewall exception. Unfortunately, this doesn't always happen automatically, and when it doesn't it can lead to applications which require Internet access not working properly. File transfer and download programs often fall into this category, and require one or more firewall ports opening to function correctly.

If you find that an application is not working correctly, check its documentation to see whether it needs firewall ports to be opened. Rather than opening individual ports for the application, the quickest solution is to give the whole application unrestricted access. You can do so by following the steps below:

Windows 7

1. Click **Start > Control Panel**.

2. Double-click **Windows Firewall**.

3. Click **Allow a program or feature through Windows Firewall**.

4. Scroll down the list of available applications, and tick the Home/Work and Public links for the application you want to allow firewall access ⑤. If the application isn't already listed, click **Allow another program**.

5. Select the program from the list, or, if it isn't listed, click **Browse**, locate the program's **.EXE** file and click **Open**, followed by **Add**.

6. Repeat step 4 for the newly added application.

7. Click **OK** ⑥.

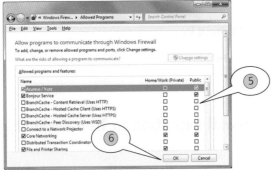

Add an exception to the firewall

Windows Vista

1. Click **Start > Control Panel**.

2. Double-click **Windows Firewall**.

3. Click **Allow a program through Windows Firewall**.

4. Scroll through the list of programs and tick the one you want to allow through the firewall.

5. If the program you want to add is not listed, click on the **Add program** button.

6. Select the program from the list, or, if it isn't listed, click **Browse**, locate the program's **.EXE** file and click **Open**, followed by **OK**.

7. Click **OK** to finish.

Windows XP

1. Click **Start > Control Panel > Windows Firewall**.

2. Click the **Exceptions** tab and look at the list of programs it contains. To create an exception for a program, click in the box next to its name.

3. If the name of the program does not appear in the box, then click the button marked **Add Program**.

4. Another dialogue box will appear that contains a list of all the programs installed on your PC. Highlight the program you wish to add to the list and click **OK**.

5. In the **Exceptions** tab, place a tick next to the program's name and click **OK**.

Cure Persistent Problems via the Advanced Configuration Settings

If you are still having problems after adding a firewall exception, the problem could be down to the way the application works. Some applications will have additional extra applications that provide some of their functionality. To overcome firewall problems, these additional applications would have to be added to the firewall exceptions list too. However, it is often quicker to just open the port or ports that the application requires.

Internet communications use one of two protocols: UDP or TCP. Check the application's documentation for the protocol used and port numbers that you need to open, then proceed as follows:

Windows 7

1. Click **Start > Control Panel**.

2. Double-click **Windows Firewall**.

3. Click **Advanced Settings**.

4. Click **Inbound Rules > New Rule**.

5. Select **Port** and click **Next**.

6. Select either **TCP** or **UDP** ⑦ and enter the port number that you would like to unblock ⑧. (You can enter multiple ports separated by a comma, or a range of ports separated by a dash).

7. Click **Next** ⑨, select **Allow the connection** and click **Next**.

8. Tick **Domain**, **Public** and **Private**, then click **Next**.

9. Enter a memorable name for the connection then click **Finish**.

10. Close the advanced firewall settings window.

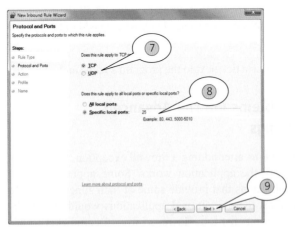

Manually configure a firewall exception

Windows Vista

1. Click **Start > Control Panel**.

2. Double-click **Windows Firewall**.

3. Click on **Allow a program through Windows Firewall**.

4. Click **Add port**.

5. Enter the name of the application that you are adding in the **Name** field. Enter the port number that you want to open in the **Port number** field.

6. Choose to open either the **TCP** or **UDP** port.

7. Click **OK**.

8. Repeat steps 1–7 for all the ports you want to add.

9. Click **OK** to finish.

Windows XP

1. Click **Start > Control Panel > Windows Firewall**.

2. Click the **Exceptions** tab, then click **Add a Port**.

3. Type a simple name into the box marked **Name**, for instance 'peer to peer'.

4. Type the number of the port you wish to open into the box marked **Port Number**.

5. Choose either **TCP** or **UDP** and click **OK**.

6. Repeat this process for every port that you wish to open.

7. Click **OK** when done.

Essential Security Steps for Router Users

If you use a router to connect to the Internet, then it will almost certainly have a built-in firewall. When enabling a firewall exception in your Windows firewall, you will also need to enable an exception in the router firewall, and configure your router to forward all the connections it receives on that port to your PC.

First, you need to find the address of your router's configuration page, as follows:

1. Press [**Windows Key**] + [**R**], type **CMD** and click **OK**.

2. At the command prompt, type **IPCONFIG**, followed by [**Enter**].

3. Make a note of the Default Gateway address.

Next, you need to set your PC's reserved IP address:

4. Open your web browser and navigate to the **Default Gateway** address you noted above.

5. Enter your router username and password – the defaults will be supplied with your router documentation.

6. Look for the **LAN Setup** screen in the **Advanced** options menu (this will be vary slightly depending on the make of router being used).

7. Give your PC a reserved IP address (this will mean that your PC gets the same IP address every time it is re-booted. Make a note of the reserved IP.

Finally, you need to set the firewall option as follows:

8. Click on the **Security** option.

9. Click on **Firewall rules** ⑩ and choose the option to add a new inbound firewall rule ⑪ (this will be vary slightly depending on the make of router being used).

10. Enter the port number of the port that you would like to open, and ensure that the traffic to the port is sent to the reserved IP address you configured in step 7.

11. Apply the changes and close your browser.

Since you often need to alter settings in your router configuration, it makes sense to bookmark the router configuration page in your browser, so that you can skip steps 1-3 above next time you need to gain access.

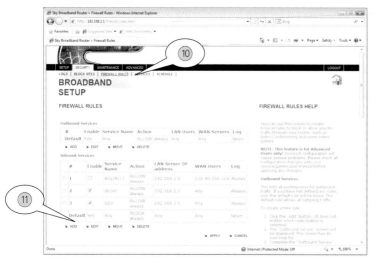

Add a new firewall rule to your router

The interface of your router will differ depending on your ISP and the router manufacturer. Check with your router's manual for the exact location of the firewall settings screen.

Check that Your Firewall is Fully Protecting Your PC

With new applications constantly requesting permission to open firewall ports, your firewall configuration can soon get out of hand, with more open ports than strictly necessary, many having been opened by applications that you no longer use. Each open port gives a hacker or virus a potential way to enter your PC, so it is essential that you periodically audit your PC to check how many ports are open.

Test the Perimeter of Your Network for Security Holes

Firstly, you should run a check on your network perimeter – this is to check the firewall between you and the Internet. If you have a router, this will check the router's firewall. If not, it will be your PC's firewall. This test will check what can be accessed from outside, and so gives you an idea of what a hacker may be able to exploit. To perform the check, follow these steps:

1. Open Internet Explorer and browse to: http://tiny.cc/tajw7.

2. Click on **Start Test > Continue**.

3. Select **TCP connect scanning (standard)** and click **Continue**.

4. Select **Scan typical vulnerable and Trojan ports** and click **Continue**.

5. The scan will run. Once complete, the results of the test will be show ⑫. If any of the ports listed are marked 'Open', then you should secure them by following the steps in the next section.

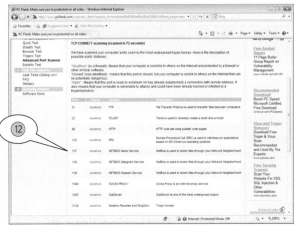

Use an online test to discover security holes in your network

Test the Internal Security of Your Home Network

If you have a home network, you should also check the firewall settings of each machine on the network. It is important that each PC has its own firewall even if you are protected by a router firewall, since if one PC becomes infected with a virus, this will prevent it from spreading.

To perform tests on each of the PCs on your home network, you should install NMAP which you can download from: http://tiny.cc/5yjpl. Install NMAP on a couple of PCs on your network, then follow the steps below to scan each machine in turn:

1. Click **Start > All Programs > NMAP > NMAP – Zenmap GUI**.

2. In the **Target** box, enter the IP address or name of the machine that you want to test ⑬.

3. Set the **Profile** drop-down list to **Intense Scan, all TCP ports** ⑭.

4. Click **Scan**.

5. When the scan is complete (which can take some time) click on the **Ports/ Hosts** tab. A list of the open ports on the tested machine will be displayed ⑮. Secure them by following the steps in the next section.

6. Repeat steps 1–5 for each machine on your home network.

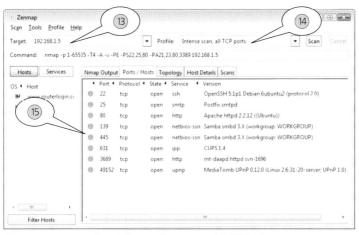

Give your network a full security scan with NMAP

If you have an outbound firewall enabled, you can test whether it is working with a tool called LeakTest, which you can download from: http://tiny.cc/rj2gf. Simply launch LeakTest and click **Test For Leaks**. If your firewall prompts you to allow the connection, choose **No**. LeakTest will report whether the firewall is secure or not.

Disable Unnecessary Applications to Minimise Security Risks

You may find that some applications add themselves to the firewall exceptions without you realising. The more applications that have exceptions in the firewall, the more at risk your computer becomes. This is because hackers will attempt to exploit bugs in running applications to gain access to your system.

The fewer security exceptions in the firewall, the fewer opportunities exist for hackers to attack your system. That is why you should regularly check your firewall settings and remove any exceptions for applications you never use, or which don't really need to access the Internet. You can disable an application as follows:

Windows 7/Vista

1. Click **Start > Control Panel**.

2. Click **Windows Firewall**.

3. Click **Allow a program or feature through Windows Firewall** (**Allow a program through Windows Firewall** in Vista).

4. Untick the applications that you want to block in the firewall.

5. Click **OK**.

Windows XP

1. Click **Start > Control Panel > Windows Firewall**.

2. Click the **Exceptions** tab.

3. Untick the program(s) that you want to block in the firewall.

4. Click **OK**.

A Quick Step for Troubleshooting Firewall Problems

If you find that you are having problems connecting to a machine even after configuring your firewall, you should first establish that the problem isn't something more serious, such as a failed network connection. To do this use the Ping tool built into Windows as follows:

1. Press [**Windows Key**] + [**R**], type **CMD** and click **OK**.

2. At the command prompt type **PING** followed by the host name or IP address of the computer that you want to test. Press [**Enter**] to execute the command.

3. If Ping reports the computer is unreachable, check your Internet connection settings and re-boot your router. If the computer does respond, then carefully check the firewall configuration as the problem is likely to be due to a misconfiguration.

Check Your Firewall for Signs of Attack

If your Internet connection slows significantly, it could be a sign that you are under prolonged attack by a hacker or virus. You should check your firewall log if lots of rejected connections are being recorded. Even if your Internet connection doesn't show any signs of slowing, it is worth regularly checking the firewall logs to see how many erroneous connections have been rejected.

Windows 7

Windows 7 records firewall information to the Event Log. You can check the log as follows:

1. Click **Start > Control Panel > Administrative Tools > Event Viewer**.

2. Click **Applications and Services Log > Microsoft > Windows > Windows Firewall with Advanced Security > Firewall** ⑯.

3. Check the events logged under firewall ⑰ – look especially for events relating to rejected connections.

Make a note of the IP addresses logged in your firewall log - if your PC has been infiltrated and serious data stolen, they could help law enforcement officials track down the offenders.

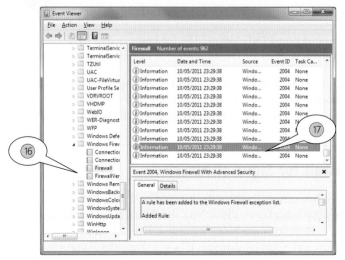

Use the Event Viewer to find firewall problems

Windows Vista

1. Click **Start > Control Panel > Administrative Tools**.

2. Select **Windows Firewall with Advanced Security**.

3. Click **Windows Firewall Properties**.

4. Click the **Customize** button next to Logging.

5. Set both of the drop-down lists to **Yes**, then click **OK**.

6. Repeat step 4 and 5 for each of the profile tabs in turn.

Windows XP

1. Click **Start > Control Panel > Windows Firewall**.

2. Click the **Advanced** tab, then click **Settings** that appears in the **Security Logging** section.

3. Place a tick in the boxes marked **Log dropped packets** and **Log successful connections**.

4. Click **OK**.

5. Open the **C:\Windows** folder and locate the file called **PFIREWALL.LOG**. Open this file to view the information recorded in the log.

Give Your XP PC Complete Security with Primedius Firewall Lite

If you use Windows XP and want to secure your PC's outbound Internet connections, you'll need to install a third party firewall as the XP firewall is only able to block inbound connections. Primedius Firewall Lite, which can secure both inbound and outbound connections, can be downloaded from http://tiny.cc/xpoj2.

With Primedius Firewall Lite installed, both inbound and outbound connections will be secured by default. When you start an application that requires either an inbound or outbound connection, you will be prompted to approve the program.

Checklist: Lock Down Your PC with Full Firewall Protection

✓ A two-way, inbound and outbound firewall will give you greatest protection from hacker and virus attacks.

✓ When an application needs to access the Internet, you must create a firewall exception to allow it access through the firewall.

✓ You should limit the number of firewall exceptions to the minimum possible, in order to reduce the possibility of attack.

✓ When an application has been uninstalled from your system, check the firewall configuration to make sure that its firewall exceptions have also been removed.

✓ Periodically run an online security check to scan your firewall for weaknesses.

3: Safely and Effectively Fight SPAM and Advertising Emails

The word SPAM is a familiar term to every email user, meaning the unsolicited advertising messages that clog up your inbox. They often contain commercial content, but can also be more deceptive and have attachments that contain viruses, worms, and Trojans; some messages might also have phishing scam hyperlinks designed to steal private information.

How is SPAM circulated?

Today, one of the spammer's favourite weapons are Botnets, or Zombie networks as they are sometimes referred to. These are hidden networks that can contain thousands of infected computers under the control of hackers for malicious purposes. Oblivious to the user, cyber criminals can remotely control these infected computers for SPAM distribution and distributed denial of service attacks (DDOS).

How do Spammers get My Email Address?

Your private email address can be obtained from a number of sources on the Internet. If you use your email address to sign-up to offers and enter competitions for example, then these compiled email databases can then be sold on – unfortunately, not everyone reads the small print on websites and assume that their private details are safe. Your email address can also be obtained by spambots. These are simple software programs that crawl the Internet looking for email addresses that have been published on public websites; examples of these are forums, social networks, or even your own website.

Should I Tell the Spammers to Stop Emailing Me?

The short answer to this is – definitely not. If you do get unwanted email then the worst thing you can do is to reply to it. The reason for this is that by replying, you are confirming that your email address is active. Spammers often bulk email to millions of possible addresses by using a technique called, Harvest Directory Attack, which is a brute force method of trying to guess addresses – most attempts produce invalid or malformed addresses, but sometimes they guess right.

You may also find that in SPAM messages there are unsubscribe links that you can click on. Unless you have subscribed to a service, or registered your details with a company, you should never click on an unsubscribe link – you're likely to get heaps more junk instead!

Crucial Steps to Protect Yourself from SPAM

Even though SPAM is a big problem that is set to get worse, there are steps that you can take to almost eradicate it from getting into your email box. Common methods you can use are:

* **Email client SPAM filtering** – modern email programs have junk email filters that can be trained to spot SPAM. You can also use keyword filtering to trap messages that have common phrases that spammers often use. Blacklists and whitelists can also be set up to provide efficient SPAM capture.

* **Anti-SPAM software** – adding another line of defence in the form of anti-SPAM software is regarded as necessary these days and will often delete the SPAM on the email server.

* **Email address munging** – this is the art of obfuscating your email address so that spambots cannot harvest it for mailing lists. Free software or online services usually use JavaScript to create code for you to use.

* **Web-based and self-destructing email addresses** – free web-based email services (Hotmail, Yahoo, etc.) have their own junk mail filters and are useful to use for one-offs such as registering as a member of websites or entering competitions. Self-destructing email addresses (e.g. http://www.sdmessage.com/) or disposable addresses (e.g. www.spamgourmet.com/) are great as SPAM blockers – good for giving to businesses or websites you don't fully trust. If you ever get SPAM, you'll know who the culprit is!

Quickly Block SPAM Using Windows Mail

Your first step in protecting yourself from getting swamped in junk email is to use your email program. Most now have features to filter out SPAM using a variety of techniques.

As well as providing great anti-SPAM features, Windows Live Mail (in Windows 7) and Windows Mail (in Vista) both have built-in SPAM filtering tools. To configure Windows Live Mail/Windows Mail, follow this step-by-step tutorial:

1. On the main screen, click on **Junk > Safety Options** or **Windows Live Mail > Options > Safety Options** (**Tools > Junk E-mail Options** in Windows Mail).

2. To add trusted email addresses to the Windows Mail whitelist, click on the **Safe Senders** tab ①.

3. Click the **Add** ② button and type in the safe email address in the text box (i.e. – user@isp.co.uk); you can also trust whole domain names too (e.g. isp@co.uk). Click the **OK** button. To speed things up in the future, click on the **Automatically add people I email to the safe senders list** option ③.

4. Click the **Blocked Senders** tab to add email addresses that you want to blacklist.

5. Click the **Add** button and type in an email address or domain name you want to block in the text box. Click **OK** to add to the blacklist.

6. Select the **International** tab to access the option to block emails that contain unwanted languages and from certain countries.

7. Click the **Blocked Top-Level Domain List** button. Select all the countries of origin you want to block or click on **Select All** for maximum protection – be careful not to block a country that you receive genuine mail from. Click **OK** to commit.

8. Click the **Blocked Encoding List** button to see a list of language encodings. Select the languages you want to filter out or click the **Select All** button for maximum protection – as with step 7, be careful not to exclude a language that one of your contacts use. Click the **OK** button to save your selections.

It makes sense to periodically check over the list of blocked senders and add any new addresses that you'd like to block, or remove people from the safe senders list if the email address is no longer used.

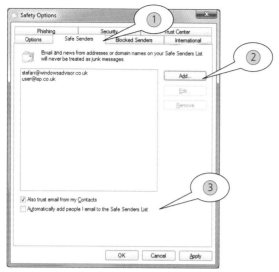

Create a list of safe senders in Windows Mail

Creating Filters in Microsoft Outlook Express 6

Although Microsoft Outlook Express 6 doesn't have as many powerful features as Windows Live Mail, it has customisable filters that can be configured to manage SPAM. These rules are then applied to all incoming mail and if a specific keyword is matched, such as in the subject line, then the email will be filtered out to a separate folder. To set up a Microsoft Outlook Express 6 subject line filter:

1. Click on the **Tools** menu, select the **Message Rules** item from the pop-up menu, followed by the **Mail** subcategory, then **New**.

2. On the New Mail Rule screen that appears, select the **Where the Subject Line Contains Specific Words** option as your condition; if you prefer, you can select another condition from the list that targets other areas of an email like the message body.

3. In the next section (Select the Actions for Your Rule), select the **Delete It** option to divert all SPAM to the Deleted folder; alternatively, you can make a separate folder that's specifically for junk email.

4. Click on the hyperlink (highlighted in blue) entitled **Contains Specific Words**. You can now enter keywords that you want to use to filter out junk – if, for example, you get SPAM with the word, Viagra, then enter this and click the **Add** button. Try variations on the same word to make your filters more effective (i.e. – V1@gra). When done adding keywords, click **OK**.

5. Finally, click **OK**. To create more rules, click on **New**, or click **OK** to return to Outlook Express 6's main screen.

yMail: a Portable SPAM-busting Email Client

If you're unhappy with the existing email program you use, or need a portable program that you can put on a USB drive, then yMail is a streamlined program with some powerful anti-SPAM features. Not only does it have built-in Bayesian SPAM filtering (an algorithm that uses statistical analysis to calculate probabilities of messages being junk), but it can also delete email messages directly from the server.

You can download this freeware program from: http://tiny.cc/ik0mo. To use yMail, follow these steps:

1. The first time you run yMail it will open a wizard to help you to configure the various settings. Click **Next** on the first screen to begin.

2. Enter your name in the first text box to identify yourself when sending email. Type in your email address in the second text box. Click **Next**.

3. On the servers screen, type in the incoming mail server address (this is the POP3 address that your Internet Service Provider (ISP) gives you). For the outgoing server address (SMTP), do the same thing using the provided text box. Click **Next**.

4. Enter your username that is required to log into your email account. Click **Next**.

5. On the final screen of the wizard, type in a user-friendly name for your account. Click the **Next** button when done. Click **Finish**.

6. Click the **Scan and Display Mail on Server** icon (green lightning) and type in your email account's password; to avoid having to type in the password every time you check mail, put a tick in the box next to the **Remember Password** option. Click the **OK** button.

7. If you have any mail on the email server, then this will be displayed in the main pane. To set up a server SPAM filter, click the **down-arrow** next to the Edit Filters icon (image of cogs) and choose **Edit Server Rules**.

8. In the Filter Name text box, type in a description – **SPAM filter 1**, for example.

9. Next, we are going to add a rule to SPAM Filter 1 to mark any message as SPAM with the word 'Viagra' in the subject line. Click on the drop-down menu displaying the word 'to' and change it to 'Subject'. Leave the next field set to Contains and in the third field, type in **Viagra**. If you want to add more rules, then tick the boxes underneath.

10. Near the bottom of the screen, you'll see the 'When Matched' option is set to **Delete From Server**; leave this setting unless you want to mark the messages as suspicious, or download them.

11. Click the **Save and Exit** button to save.

12. Click the **Scan and Display Mail on Server** icon (green lightning) again to see the effect of the SPAM filter that has been set up. The status column should now change from a pass to a fail ④ if there are any messages that match the filter we have just set up.

13. Finally, click the **Download Mail and Delete SPAM** icon (you may need to click the down arrow beside the envelope icon) to only download the good email.

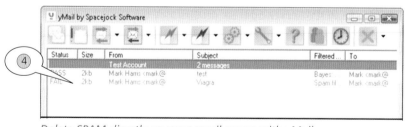

Delete SPAM directly on your email server with yMail

It will take a while to add all of the rules that you need to defeat SPAM, but once you have your configuration working you should find that your SPAM level becomes much more manageable.

Defeat the Spammer with Anti-SPAM Software

To complement the anti-SPAM controls that your email client has, it is advisable to also have a dedicated software program that can filter junk email. This second line of defence, in many cases, can delete SPAM even before it's downloaded from the email server.

If you've got a single email address that you want to protect from SPAM, then MailWasher Free is the ideal solution. Because this free program deletes SPAM straight from the email server (typically your Internet Service Provider's), it also saves you from having to download large messages that may have dangerous payloads via attachments.

You can download this invaluable program from: http://tiny.cc/j9tz4. Once installed, follow this short tutorial to get up and running:

1. The first time MailWasher Free is run, an import wizard scans your computer for compatible email programs that contain account information. Select the account you wish to use and click **Accept**, followed by **OK**. If you need to add the information manually, then click on the **Tools** menu via the main screen and select **General Options** from the menu list.

2. Click **Email Accounts** in the left pane, followed by **Add Account**. Click on **OK** to set up a POP3 account (normal type for ISP-based emails).

3. For incoming mail, type in a user-friendly name in the **Account Name** text box. Fill in the **POP3 server address** details (look this up in your email client or consult your ISP's website). Type in the username and password in the text boxes provided. Keep the **Remember Password** option ticked to save having to input the password every time you check mail.

4. Click **General Options** in the left pane and click on the **Load MailWasher Free on Startup** option to run it every time Windows starts. Click **OK** to finish configuring MailWasher Free.

5. Click on the **Check Mail** icon on the main screen. If you have new messages waiting on the email server, then they will be displayed in the main pane.

6. MailWasher Free takes a while to learn what SPAM is and so if you see an unwanted email, then click the red icon in the Action column ⑤.

7. To add the email address to the blacklist, right-click the message and select **Add to Blacklist** from the pop-up menu. To add a whole domain, choose the **Add Domain to the Blacklist** option.

8. Finally, to process the list of emails on the server click the **Process Mail** icon. All good emails will be downloaded by your email client and the SPAM won't even make it to your PC.

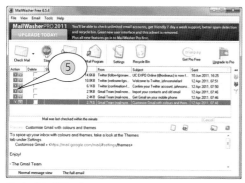

Train MailWasher Free to recognise SPAM

POPFile: A SPAM Filter Compatible with Almost Every Email Program

Another type of software program that you can use in the quest to eliminate SPAM is to use a POP3 email proxy. This sits between your existing email client and the mail server. POPFile uses Bayesian SPAM filtering to effectively filter out SPAM. As the system learns, it becomes more accurate at classifying SPAM.

To set up an email proxy on your system, install POPFile from: http://tiny.cc/ d5u2v. To configure your email client and POPFile, do the following:

1. To check that POPFile is running, type **http://127.0.0.1:8080** in your web browser. The POPFile control center should be displayed.

2. Click the **Buckets** ⑥ tab to view POPFile's bucket configuration ⑦. By default there is already a SPAM bucket, but you can add more buckets if you like by using the maintenance section – useful for categorising your email (i.e. – friends, family, etc.).

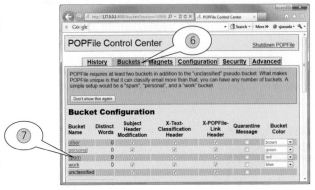

Create email categories with POPFile

If the POPFile installer hasn't automatically set up your email client to point to it, then go to your email program's POP3 account settings and enter 127.0.0.1 as the POP3 (incoming) server address – make a note of the existing POP3 address (e.g. mail.myisp.net) before you overwrite it. In the username field, insert the old server address that you made a note of in front of the username that's already present, separating the two with a colon (i.e. mail.myisp.net:username).

Every message that POPFile inspects will have a tag in front of the subject name. For example, a SPAM message's subject name will have the tag, [SPAM], inserted before the subject name. You can then create a filter in your email program to move the identified SPAM to the junk folder (or even a new custom folder, called SPAM, for example).

To train POPFile to recognise SPAM, you'll need to manually classify emails to start off with. To reclassify a wrongly identified email:

1. Double-click on the Octopus icon in your system tray if POPFile's interface isn't displayed in your browser; alternatively, type **127.0.0.1:8080** in your browser's address bar.

2. Click on the **History** tab. You'll see a list of messages that have been received with a classification next to each one. To change a setting, click the drop-down menu and choose a classification.

3. Click on the **Reclassify** button to process. Remember, it will take some time to train POPFile, so be patient.

Protect Your Email Address Using SPAM Bot Blocker

The art of munging is defined as cloaking your email address in order to prevent it from being harvested by spambots. If you've got a website, or post messages on forums, then SPAM Bot Blocker (which you can download from: http://tiny.cc/bvuyz) will automatically generate the code you need. Follow these steps to munge your email address:

1. Type your email address in the text box.

2. Ensure that the JavaScript option is selected for maximum protection and click **Go**.

3. Click the **Copy to Clipboard** button to easily paste it into your web page code.

Check that Your Email is Ultra-secure and Protected Against Mail-borne Malware

Email is an incredibly useful means of communication, but it is also a common means of spreading viruses. Other potential problems exist in the form of phishing emails which can be used to attempt to extract personal information from recipients. Many email clients include spam and phishing filters that can help to combat these problems, but tests can reveal just how effective your protection is:

1. Pay a visit to the GFI Email Security Testing Zone at http://tiny.cc/54b07, scroll down the page and tick the boxes next to each of the tests listed.

2. At the bottom of the page, enter your name and email address before clicking the **Test my email system!** button.

3. A series of emails will be sent to you, some of which have attachments while others will attempt to create files on your desktop.

If any of the tests are unsuccessful they will have been automatically blocked. However, if they are successfully executed, your virus and malware protection may not be properly configured. It is worth checking the spam filtering settings of your email client to ensure that they are configured to block suspicious messages – the exact process varies between programs, so check the help file for details.

Checklist: Prevent SPAM from Clogging Your Inbox

✓ Never reply to a SPAM email, as this will alert the spammers to the fact that your email address is active.

✓ Configure SPAM blocking software to automatically detect and filter out SPAM messages.

✓ If an unsolicited email arrives offering something that is too good to be true, it probably is – ignore it.

✓ Only use your email address in situations when you know it won't fall into the hands of spammers.

✓ If you start to receive a lot of SPAM messages that seem to come from someone you know, it is likely that their email account has been hacked and their address book stolen. Let them know about the problem, preferably by a means other than email.

✓ If other people start to receive SPAM messages that look like they've come from you, give your PC a full anti-virus scan to ensure that no malicious software is hijacking your email account.

✓ Links at the bottom of SPAM messages that claim to unsubscribe you from the spammer's mailing list should also be avoided, as these too confirm that your email address is active.

5: Spyware: Don't Give Data Snoopers a Chance

Knowing the likely threats to your PC's security that you can come across on the Internet is half of the battle. Once you're in the habit of looking for suspicious websites and online scams, you will be able to easily avoid the great majority of them. Spyware and other snooping software are major threats to your online security. The table below summarises the threats that you are likely to encounter:

Threat	Discription
Adware	Adware is a term used to describe software that you install on your PC that is supported by advertising. Very often this takes the form of free or shareware software that displays adverts while you are using it, either in the main application window or in separate pop-up windows. While this sounds relatively benign the constant adverts can be quite annoying, and some adware also includes spyware or other unwanted software that is installed to your PC without you knowing about it, or having any choice regarding the installation. Unlike spyware and viruses, adware is often explicitly installed by the user, as it is bundled with an application that the user wants to install.
Spyware	Spyware is malicious software that's installed on your PC without your knowledge, and is designed to monitor or take over your interaction with Windows and report back to an Internet server controlled by the spyware's author. Spyware infections exist that can monitor and collect many different types of personal information, from online banking passwords to the websites that you visit most often. The latter is often used to target the adverts that an adware infection displays to an individual user.
Clickjacking	Clickjacking is the latest threat to emerge online, and is due to recently discovered weaknesses in many popular web browsers. Clickjacking allows a hacker to force a user to click on an invisible link without the user knowing, which then installs malicious software secretly to the user's PC. It works by placing a link over a legitimate URL. When you click on it the hidden link is activated instead.

Of course, spyware and adware infections often go hand in hand with viruses, and many viruses that infect your PC will also download and install other spyware and adware infections on to your computer. For full details of how to deal with virus infections, see Chapter 1.

The 4 Tell-tale Signs of a Serious Spyware Infection

Many spyware infections are intended to be transparent to the user, so that they can remain undetected on your PC for as long as possible. Adware infections are easier to spot, since their primary purpose is to display pop-up adverts on your desktop. However, there are a few tell-tale signs of infection that you can look out for which indicate both adware and spyware infections:

- **Pop-up adverts** – adverts pop-up at random times on your desktop, usually in a browser window and often advertising products of a dubious nature. These pop-up ads can occur even when your web browser is not open. On no account click on any of these adverts.

- **Changes to settings** – settings on your PC, most commonly in Internet Explorer, are changed without you doing anything, and revert to the changed setting even when you try to change them back. A setting that is often changed in this way is Internet Explorer's home page.

- **Extra web browser components added** – extra tools are present in Internet Explorer which you haven't added yourself. These can often take the form of browser toolbars, and will be listed in the browser add-ons screen accessed by clicking **Cog** icon > **Manage Addons** (**Tools** > **Manage Addons** in older versions of IE).

- **Your computer is sluggish** – your PC may suddenly start to take a long time to boot up as the result of an infection, or may run very slowly. This is due to the malware or spyware infections taking up valuable system resources which mean they aren't available for your regular applications.

If your computer is running sluggishly, you can quickly check what's going on in the Task Manager, simply press [**Ctrl**] + [**R**], type **TASKMGR** and press [**Enter**]. The Task Manager shows you a list of all the processes that are running on your PC. Any process that is taking up a large percentage of your CPU (Central Processing Unit) even though no applications are running, can be indicative of infection.

Iif there are any you don't recognise the names of, you can look them up on the Process Library website: www.processlibrary.com/.

Quickly Combat Spyware with Spybot – Search and Destroy

There are lots of free tools available to remove spyware infections from your system, and knowing which to choose can be difficult. One of the main problems is that hackers use bogus spyware removal tools to actually infect your system further. We'd recommend that you use the excellent Spybot – Search and Destroy, which you can download from http://tiny.cc/ycpgo. Once installed, to scan Windows for infection and clean up your system, follow the steps below:

1. Click **Create registry backup**.

2. Click **Next**, then click **Search for Updates**.

3. Click **Continue**, select all of the download options, and then click **Download**.

4. Click **Exit** after the download is complete and switch to the main window.

5. On the main window, click **Check for problems** ①. A full system scan will begin that will last for some time.

6. Click **Fix selected problems** ② > **Yes** > **OK**.

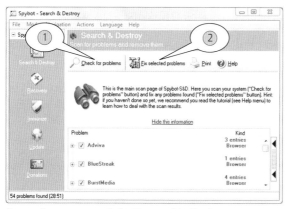

Removing spyware infections with Spybot

After repairing problems, you can use Spybot to immunise your system against future attacks, by blocking some of the attack methods (called attack vectors in computer security parlance). To do so, follow the steps below:

7. Click on **Immunize** in the left-hand panel.

8. Ensure that all of the immunisation options listed are ticked.

9. Click on the **Immunize** button.

Removing Adware Infections with Ad-Aware 2011

Adware is often installed alongside shareware tools that use the adverts to generate income for the developers. Unfortunately, removing the offending shareware tool will not always remove the adware software that accompanied it. We would recommend that you use Ad-Aware, which you can download from: http://tiny.cc/ydzfh, to regularly scan your PC and remove adware infections.

Beware after using Ad-Aware: removing adware infections can stop the shareware programs that they came with from working properly. This shouldn't matter too much; since the shareware tools have installed infections on your systems, it is best not to use them anyway. To remove adware infections:

1. Open Ad-Aware 2011.

2. Click **Web Update** in the left-hand column to download the latest adware definitions for Ad-Aware.

3. Once the download is complete click on **OK** on the window that pops up.

4. Click **Scan** ③ then select **Full Scan**. The scanning process can take some time so be patient.

5. Once the scan is complete any infections that have been removed will be shown in the main screen ④.

6. Click **Done**.

If you find a particular tool has stopped working after running Ad-Aware, then uninstall the tool completely using the Control Panel.

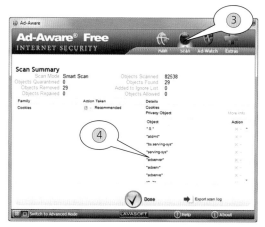

Removing adware infections with Ad-Aware

Beware of the Latest Internet Security Threat

Clickjacking is the latest threat to strike the Internet. The security researchers who discovered Clickjacking have given out very few details of the nature of the threat, but it is believed that attacks can occur on any website, even legitimate ones. Consequently there is very little software available to help prevent against Clickjacking attacks – your regular spyware and phishing tools won't help here.

Fortunately one solution does exist, but it is only available for Firefox users. If you are worried about becoming victim of a Clickjacking attack, we would advise that you switch to using the latest version of Firefox (which you can download from: http://tiny.cc/cg3se), and install the NoScript add-on (which you can download from: http://tiny.cc/vpwkv).

Once installed, the plugin will block all scripts from all websites unless you explicitly add them to your whitelist. It also features a tool called ClearClick to explicitly guard against Clickjacking. You can add sites to your whitelist as follows:

1. Click on the **Options** button in the NoScript toolbar at the bottom of the screen.

2. Click **Options** > **Whitelist**, enter the address of the website that you want to allow and click **Allow**.

3. Click **OK**.

To enable ClearClick, follow the steps below:

1. Click on the **Options** button in the NoScript toolbar at the bottom of the screen.

2. Click **Options > Embeddings**.

3. Tick the options **Forbid <IFRAME>** and **Apply these restrictions to trusted sites too**, then click **OK**.

7 Quick Steps to Manually Remove Spyware Infections

Spyware infections that attack your PC will usually not be able to function unless they place entries in the registry which cause them to be activated when Windows starts up. Using a tool called HijackThis, which you can download from: http://tiny.cc/yzgfn, you can detect any anomalous registry entries present on your PC, and use them to trace the spyware infections on your PC.

Unfortunately, HijackThis doesn't identify spyware threats for you – it only shows you how your PC's configuration deviates from the norm, and therefore where your PC could potentially be infected. However, this allows you to find anything that could potentially be a threat, but it requires a bit more detective work to find out exactly what each item discovered is. In the seven-point plan below, we will show you how to do this:

Step 1: Scan your PC with HijackThis

Install the HijackThis tool and then follow the steps below in order to analyse your PC:

1. Click **Start > All Programs > HijackThis > HijackThis**.

2. Click **Do a system scan and save a logfile**.

3. Once the scan has completed, the log file detailing all of the potential infections found will be opened. **Click File > Save As** and choose to save the file to your desktop.

 If you find problems running HijackThis on Windows 7 or Vista, then click **Start > All Programs > HiJackThis**, then right-click on **HiJackThis** and either choose **Run as administrator**, or click **Properties > Compatibility**, tick **Run this program as Administrator** and click **OK**.

Once the log file has been created you need to analyse the potential infections found ⑤. The log file first lists the processes that are running on your PC, and then the registry entries that could potentially be related to spyware infections. If you are able, print out the HijackThis log for reference.

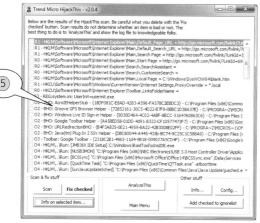

Scanning for spyware infections with HijackThis

In order to analyse your log file you will need to search for each item online. Opening your web browser and searching for each item on Google should tell you whether it is a spyware problem or not. However, a website called http://hjt.networktechs.com/ provides an online tool to automatically analyse your entire log for you. To use it, follow the steps below:

1. Open Notepad from **Start** > **All Programs** > **Accessories** > **Notepad**, and then open your hijackthis.log file using **File** > **Open**.

2. Press [**Ctrl**] + [**A**] then [**Ctrl**] + [**C**] to copy the contents of the log file to the clipboard.

3. Open your web browser and browse to: http://hjt.networktechs.com/

4. Click into the text field at the bottom of the page, then press [**Ctrl**] + [**V**] to paste the contents of the log.

5. Click **Parse**. Once the analysis has completed, you will see a page similar to the screenshot below ⑥.

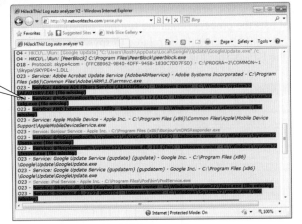

Analysing your HijackThis log online

Potential problems are marked in red, and should be deleted. Make a note of any items marked in red, which we will remove later. You can also search for any red entries using Google to discover more details about them.

If you have spyware infections that were detected using the Spybot – Search and Destroy tool, but which it couldn't remove, use the names of the infections noted earlier to search for details of the infection's file and registry settings. Entering the names of the infections into Google will bring up many pages showing details of the infections.

Step 2: Disable your PC's Internet connection

Before you remove infections from your PC, you should disable your Internet connection to prevent any other infections from installing themselves on to your PC. To disable your connection, follow the steps below:

1. Press **[Windows Key] + [R]**, type **NCPA.CPL** and click **OK**.

2. Right-click on your **Internet Connection** adaptor (or **Local Area Connection** adaptor if you connect to the Internet through a local area network) and choose **Disable** from the pop-up menu.

Step 3: Make a complete registry backup

Before you remove any detected infections from your PC you should make a full registry backup by creating a System Restore Point that will allow you to revert your PC to a working configuration if anything goes wrong.

If you find that there is a problem with an application on your PC after manually removing spyware infections, you can either revert to the restore point, or try uninstalling then re-installing the problem application.

To create a System Restore Point, follow the steps below:

Windows 7

1. Click **Start** > **Control Panel** > **System**.

2. Click on the link **System Protection**, then click **Create**.

3. Enter a name for your restore point, then click **OK**.

4. Once the restore point had been created, click **Close** > **OK**.

Windows Vista

1. Click **Start**, right-click on **Computer**, and click **Properties**.

2. Click on the link **System protection**.

3. Select your **C:** drive from the list of available drives ⑦ and click **Create** ⑧.

4. Enter a name for your restore point and click **Create**.

5. Click **OK** > **OK**.

When creating a restore point, try to give it a name that will make it easy to remember exactly why you created it, e.g. "Prior to removing spyware".

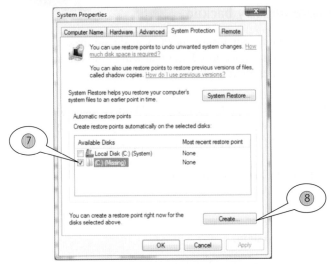

Creating a restore point in Windows Vista

Windows XP

1. Click **Start > All Programs > Accessories > System Tools > System Restore**.

2. Select **Create a restore point** and click **Next**.

3. Type a name for your restore point (e.g. **Spyware Removal**) and then click **Create**.

4. Click **Close** once the restore point has been created.

Step 4: Remove the infected settings from the registry

Next, we have to remove any registry entries marked as 'Questionable' or 'Dangerous'. This should be done in Windows Safe Mode, to ensure that none of the infections that are to be removed will actually be running in the background. To re-boot into Safe Mode, follow the steps below:

1. Re-boot your computer.

2. As the PC restarts, hold down the **[F8]** key until the Advanced Options menu appears.

3. Select **Safe Mode** using the [**Up Arrow**] and [**Down Arrow**] keys, and then press [**Enter**].

Once in Safe Mode, you should remove the problem registry entries found by HijackThis, plus any discovered by Spybot which couldn't be removed, as follows:

1. Press [**Windows Key**] + [**R**], type **REGEDIT** and press [**Enter**].

2. Navigate to the first problem registry key identified in your HijackThis log (you will probably need to look at your HijackThis log in conjunction with your analysis report to determine the full path to the problem registry entries).

3. In the right-hand panel, right-click on each problem registry entry ⑨ in turn and click **Delete**.

4. Repeat steps 2–3 for each registry problem identified.

5. When done, close the registry editor with **File > Exit**.

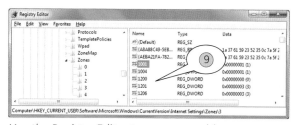

Use the Registry Editor to remove problems

Ensure that you make a note of any file paths listed in the registry entries you delete, as these files will correspond to the spyware infections and will need to be removed in the next step.

Step 5: Delete the infected files from your hard drive

After removing problem registry entries from your system, you must next get rid of the files that the spyware infections have placed on your hard drive.

Use the list of files you collated in step 4, along with the problem files identified in your HijackThis log and any identified by Spybot which couldn't be automatically removed, to delete the files as follows:

1. First, make sure that hidden and system files are visible. Open Windows Explorer and click **Tools > Folder Options**.

2. Click on the **View** tab.

3. Untick the option **Hide protected operating system files (recommended)**.

4. Select the option **Show hidden files, folders and drives** (**Show hidden files and folders** in older Windows versions).

5. Click **Apply > OK** to apply the changes.

6. Navigate to the first problem file identified, select the file then hold down [**Shift**] and press [**Delete**]. This will cause the file to be deleted immediately rather than placing it in the Recycle Bin.

7. Repeat step 6 for each problem file identified. Once complete, re-boot your PC.

Step 6: Repair the hosts file

The Windows hosts file is the location where Windows stores frequently used Internet host and site names. When Windows needs to find the Internet IP address of a certain website or computer, it consults the hosts file first, before checking with your Internet Service Provider's (ISP's) Domain Name System (DNS) server.

Many spyware infections will exploit this feature of Windows to maliciously divert you to hacker websites when you use the Internet. A spyware infection might, for example, list the IP address of a hacker site alongside the web address of your online bank, meaning that when you try to access the bank's website you are in fact diverted to the hacker website.

If you have removed spyware infections from your PC, you should also check that no malicious entries have been placed in the hosts file, leaving you susceptible to future attack. To check, follow the steps below:

1. Click **Start > All Programs > Accessories**, right-click on **Notepad** and choose **Run as administrator** (XP users, just click **Notepad**).

2. Click **File > Open**.

3. Change the Text Document drop-down to **All Files**.

4. Navigate to and double-click on the file **C:\Windows\System32\drivers\ etc\hosts**.

5. When the hosts file opens, check for any suspicious entries ⑩. If you haven't made any changes to the file yourself previously, you should see only one line in XP (**127.0.0.1 localhost**) or no lines in Windows 7/Vista. If you see any other entries, delete them.

6. Click **File > Save**, then **File > Exit**.

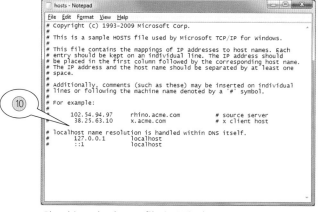

Checking the hosts file in Windows XP

Step 7: Re-enable your Internet connection

After you have removed all infections present on your PC, you should re-enable your Internet connection as follows:

1. Press [**Windows Key**] + [**R**], type **NCPA.CPL** and click **OK**.

2. Right-click on your **Internet Connection** adaptor (or **Local Area Connection** adaptor if you connect to the Internet through a local area network) and choose **Enable** from the pop-up menu.

Once you have completed these steps you should have manually removed all of the files and registry settings associated with the spyware infections found on your computer.

Check that Your PC is No Longer Infected with a Comprehensive Online Scan

Once all of the spyware infections on your PC have been manually removed, you should give your PC a full scan to ensure that no more infections are present using the online Trend Micro scanning tool. To do so, follow these steps:

1. Open your web browser and navigate to the website: http://housecall. trendmicro.com/uk/.

2. Click on **Start Scan** (choose either the 32-bit or 64-bit scan depending on your Windows version).

3. Follow the prompts from your browser to run the scan.

4. Accept the terms and conditions and click **Next**.

5. Click **Scan Now** ⑪.

6. Leave the system scan to complete and choose to remove any infections that are found.

Use HouseCall to give your PC a full security scan

 Hopefully, the scan will give your PC a clean bill of health. If any infections are detected, make a note of them and search for details of the files and registry settings that they create on your PC. Follow steps 1–7 of the manual spyware removal plan we have described to remove the infections.

Test the Effectiveness of Your Malware Protection

Because malware takes so many forms, it can be difficult to test for all eventualities, but Spycar provides a number of tests to allow you to evaluate your anti-malware software and check whether it is working or not:

1. Pay a visit to the Spycar website at http://tiny.cc/vkicv and scroll down the page to view a list of the available tests.

2. Click each of the **here** links in the **Autostart Tests** – there are six in total – and the site will attempt to make a series of changes to your registry.

3. Now click each of the **here** links in the **Internet Explorer Config Change Tests** section – there are ten in total.

4. Finally, click the **here** link under the **Network Config Change Tests** section to perform the last test. The fake malware files will attempt to make changes to your system settings.

5. If your malware protection is working, each of the attempted changes should be blocked.

6. Undo any changes that have slipped through the net by clicking the **here** link in the **Results and Clean-up** section – this will display the results of the tests and reverse any changes that were made. If your security software tries to block this link, allow it to run as an exception.

Any tests that managed to beat your defences may indicate that your chosen malware protection is insufficient.

Checklist: Avoid Spyware Infections that Can Steal Sensitive Data

✓ Only install software from reputable sources – some bogus software carries with it spyware infections.

✓ When spyware infections refuse to budge from your system, remove them manually.

✓ Give your spyware software a full test to check that it is working properly.

✓ Run a regular scan of your PC to check for spyware and adware infections.

✓ Protect yourself against Clickjacking infections with the NoScript add-on for Firefox.

5: Phishing: 100% Protection Against Internet Fraud

One of the problems with phishing scams, aside from the purpose they were designed for, is the fact that they work by tricking victims into believing they are dealing with websites or emails which are connected to well known legitimate organisations – this often includes banks and building societies as well as famous websites such as eBay and PayPal.

Victims are lured into handing over personal details such as the credentials needed to log into an online account or even bank account details. Visitors are directed to phishing websites in a number of ways, but the most common is to send out links via email or instant messenger or to include a link to a fake site on another page.

The fake sites have been designed to very closely mimic the genuine sites they are impersonating, and as such it can be difficult to quickly identity scams at a glance. That said, there are still a number of techniques that can be used to distinguish between a genuine site and a fake one.

Double-check the address of the website that is currently loaded before parting with any information. As well as mimicking the layout and appearance of genuine sites, fake websites often have very similar addresses to their real counterparts – such as www.ebat.com instead of www.ebay.com.

Any web pages that are used for financial transactions should be secure. This can be checked in a number of ways, the first being to ensure that the page's URL starts with https://. Secondly, when a secure page is loaded, a padlock icon should be visible in either the address bar or status bar depending on which web browser is being used, and this indicates that the company that owns the website has been checked and confirmed as genuine.

By clicking or double-clicking the padlock icon, it is possible to view additional information about the company that holds the security certificate, including their registered address. Such verification by the security company VeriSign should be sufficient to be sure that the site is genuine. If no secure web page is available for making a transaction, it is possible that the site is not genuine.

Many fake websites are very cleverly designed so that certain links on a fake page direct visitors to pages on a genuine website. For example, a victim may visit a fake banking site, but when the 'About Us' link is clicked, a page from the genuine banking site is displayed. It is because of tricks like this that it is important to check the validity of all links you intend to use on a page – just hover the mouse cursor over a link, and the address of the destination page will be displayed in the web browser status bar.

Configure Internet Explorer's Phishing Filter to Boost Security

Recent versions of Microsoft Internet Explorer have a built-in phishing filter which can be used to automatically detect fake websites. In Internet Explorer 9 and 8, this feature is known as the SmartScreen Filter and the first step is to ensure that this tool is enabled:

1. Launch Internet Explorer and click **Tools** (the cog icon) > **Internet Options**.

2. Move to the **Advanced** tab and scroll to the bottom of the **Settings** list.

3. Ensure that the box labelled **Enable SmartScreen Filter** is ticked and click **OK**.

Whenever a phishing website is detected, a warning will appear on-screen informing you that the page is unsafe. Individual pages can also be checked manually by clicking the **Safety** toolbar button and selecting **SmartScreen Filter > Check This Website**, from the menu that appears. The tool will also block the download of any files which have been reported as being unsafe.

The phishing filter found in Internet Explorer 7 is still very effective at detecting and blocking access to suspicious pages, but users of IE7 or earlier should upgrade to IE8 or IE9 if possible, to get a better level of protection.

Enable Extra Security Protection in Firefox and Opera

It is not just Internet Explorer that offers protection against phishing websites – similar security features can be found in Firefox, Opera and a number of other web browsers.

In Firefox, for example, phishing and malware Protection should be enabled by default, offering protection against fake websites and dangerous downloads by making use of a constantly updated list of malicious sites. To ensure that the security features are enabled, use the following steps:

1. Launch Firefox and click **Firefox > Options** (**Tools > Options** in older versions).

2. Move to the **Security** tab and ensure that the three boxes at the top of the dialogue are all ticked ① before clicking **OK** ②.

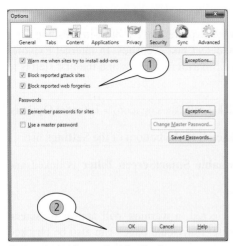

Secure your browsing in Firefox

A similar set of security tools is also available in the Opera browser in the form of Fraud Protection, which works in much the same way as for other browsers. Again, the feature should be enabled by default, but it is worth checking to be on the safe side.

1. Launch Opera and click **Tools > Preferences**.

2. Move to the **Advanced** tab and select **Security** from the left-hand section.

3. Ensure that the box labelled **Enable Fraud Protection** is ticked and then click **OK**.

Use McAfee SiteAdvisor to Avoid Scam Sites

Another way to avoid phishing scams is to turn to a dedicated security tool such as McAfee SiteAdvisor. This free tool can be downloaded from: http://tiny.cc/omj1w. Just like the phishing filters found in web browsers, SiteAdvisor works in much the same way as anti-virus software, relying on a list of reported phishing sites which is constantly referred to as sites are visited and checked for safety.

The tool works in conjunction with the Yahoo! search engine, but this does not stop you from using other search engines – although it should be remembered that sites will not be checked when using something other than Yahoo!.

1. Start the installation process and indicate whether the Yahoo! Toolbar should also be installed.

2. Leave the box labelled **Enable Secure Search** ticked.

3. By selecting the first of the next three options, sites which are thought to be dangerous will be hidden from search results. Select the second option to show all results along with a safety rating.

4. Leave Yahoo! as the default search engine and click **Finish**.

Installing the program will install add-ons for Internet Explorer, Firefox and Google Chrome – the tool is not currently compatible with other browsers. When you next want to search the Internet, type your search term in the search box ③ and press [**Enter**].

Securely search the Web with Site Advisor

Depending on the options that have been selected, the search results will be filtered in one of two ways. If sites of all ratings have been disabled, and 'red sites' have been blocked, only results that are known to be safe will be listed. If 'red sites' have been enabled along with the option to display sites of all ratings, search results will be shown with a traffic light rating system, with green indicating that a site is safe, yellow that it is potentially dangerous, and red that the site poses a threat.

Take Additional Steps to Stay Secure Online

A very common way for phishing sites to attract visitors is to send out junk email purporting to originate from legitimate organisations such as banks. Other techniques include emails which suggest that another person has attempted to access one of your online accounts, and asks you to provide your username and password to verify your details.

In reality, the vast majority of such emails are likely to be fakes. Banks will not send out emails asking for personal information, and the same is true of most other organisations. If you receive an email of this nature, do not click any links it contains. Instead, to check whether you need to take any action with the site from which the email is said to have been sent, visit the site directly by typing the URL into the address bar of your web browser, or use a bookmark you know to be genuine. You can then log into your account to see if any steps need to be taken.

While there is no getting away from the fact that there are numerous dangers associated with connecting to the Internet, there is no need for undue concern. Providing care is taken, and with the assistance of one of the various security tools that are available, it is possible to stay safe online and avoid the risk of falling victim to the numerous scams that exist. Scam websites are usually detected very quickly, and will therefore be detected by anti-phishing filters, but if you are in any doubt about a particular site, simply leave it alone.

Checklist: Be on the Lookout for Phishing Attacks

✓ Phishing attacks use cleverly constructed fake websites to fool you into parting with your hard-earned cash.

✓ Using a phishing filter will help you quickly spot phishing attacks.

✓ Configure your web browser's security settings to protect yourself against illegitimate websites.

6: Protect Your Computer Against Hidden Rootkits

The latest threat to your Windows PC's security is the rootkit. This is a special software program, often used to conceal traditional Trojan and virus programs, by hiding them from the Windows system. The term derives from the Unix operating system, where rootkits were originally modified versions of common programs designed to give the user access to resources they normally would not.

Usually, a virus will be present on your PC in the form of a file or set of files. Virus and spyware writers go to great lengths to hide their malicious files, for example, by burying them deeply within the Windows folder file structure, but they are still contained in normal files and therefore can still be found and deleted.

Rootkits are designed to intercept Windows system calls in order to hide files; for example, when Windows Explorer asks for the files contained in a particular directory so that they can be displayed on-screen, the rootkit can intercept the call and return a list of all of the files in the directory except for the malicious one that it is hiding.

Rootkits can strike from unlikely sources

One of the most famous cases of rootkit infection was not even designed to cause malicious damage to your PC. In 2005, Sony BMG included a rootkit on their music CDs that surreptitiously installed itself on your PC when the CD was played. Rather than hiding a virus or other malicious software, the rootkit was designed to install and hide Sony's copy-protection software, to prevent the CD from being copied.

This caused an outcry due to the fact that Sony didn't tell customers that this would happen when they tried to play the CD on their PC, and that the rootkit introduced a number of security vulnerabilities to Windows that would allow a virus to more easily infect a system. The rootkit also drained PC performance when a CD was playing, even if it wasn't a Sony protected CD. A number of lawsuits resulted against Sony, forcing them to recall the CDs and issue a removal kit to remove the rootkit from infected PCs.

How rootkits infect your PC

Like many other types of virus and spyware, very often rootkits take advantage of unsuspecting users to install themselves on a PC. Executable email attachments, Internet downloads, and spyware pop-ups are all favourite mechanisms for rootkit distribution. Rootkit writers very often masquerade their software as something that a user will want to install in order to get the user to inadvertently install it on their PC.

As with any other virus, be careful when browsing the Internet and avoid installing software that you cannot confirm the source of. Be especially wary of pop-up Windows that claim that your PC is infected and tell you to install their software to remove the problem. Almost always these types of message are scams to get you to install something nasty.

Due to the way that virus checkers and anti-spyware programs work, they will not always find rootkits when they are introduced on to your PC. Later in this chapter, we will look at some of the best free rootkit removal and scanning software available.

Different Types of Rootkit

There are four different kinds of rootkit, catagorised by the way they infect your PC. The different types are:

- **Virtualized** – virtualized rootkits operate at the lowest level of system operation. They work by subverting the way that the PC's operating system loads, loading themselves first. Then, once resident in memory, loading the operating system as a virtualized machine. These are currently only at the 'proof of concept stage' and there are no malicious ones currently in the wild.

- **Kernel level** – kernel level rootkits work by inserting their own modified code into the Windows Kernel, so that they can take over certain key Windows functions. Very often these rootkits are installed as device drivers and can cause a great deal of damage to a running system. Kernel rootkits can be especially dangerous because they can be difficult to detect without appropriate software.

- **Library level** – these rootkits very often patch system libraries (collections of program code used by numerous applications) to introduce their own versions of the code, hiding information about the attacker.

- **Application level** – application level rootkits replace a common application with a modified version, designed for malicious purposes. For example, the MS-DOS DIR command could be replaced with a version that doesn't report a certain malicious file when it is used in a certain directory.

How to Spot a Rootkit Infection on Your PC

Because rootkits are designed to hide themselves, it is unlikely that you will see any outward signs that you are infected. It's much more likely that you will see activity from the virus or Trojan that the rootkit is designed to mask.

This will cover the usual symptoms of a virus infection including random crashes and error messages, constant network access even when the PC is idle, a modified web browser start page and files being mysteriously deleted. But, unlike a normal virus infection, your anti-virus software will report nothing untoward, because the rootkit is hiding the virus from the checker.

If this is the case then you need some of the specialist rootkit removal software covered in the next section.

Root out Rootkits with these Free Specially-designed Programs

All of the types of rootkit mentioned above can be very difficult to detect, often thwarting traditional anti-virus software. Because rootkits are specifically designed to hide themselves, specialist anti-rootkit software is required to remove them.

The table below lists some of the best free rootkit removal software available on the market, all of which can be downloaded using the links shown in the table.

Application	Discription	Link
Sophos AntiRootkit	Perform a deep level scan of your system for hidden rootkits, and remove any found.	http://tiny.cc/ph6v3
SanityCheck	Check for any programs making use of Kernel hooks, a common tactic used by rootkits.	http://tiny.cc/vb346
Sysinternals Rootkit Revealer	Perform twin level scans of your system's hard drive to find discrepancies caused by rootkits (XP only).	http://tiny.cc/y6a53

Although a number of the tools listed in the table above do the same thing, very often rootkits will exploit a particular weakness that only some of the scanning tools recognise. Therefore, we recommend that if you suspect that you have a rootkit infecting your PC that you try a combination of different tools, as a single tool may not find the specific infection.

Reveal Secret Keyloggers with Sophos AntiRootkit

Sophos AntiRootkit is one of the best rootkit removal applications around and it can be installed to a USB stick so that you can take it with you, and use it to clean up any infected PC. Once you've installed the tool to a folder on your memory stick, you can use it as follows:

1. Right-click on the file **SARGUI.EXE** and choose **Run as administrator** (XP users, just double-click on the file).

2. Ensure the options **Windows registry** and **Local hard drives** are ticked.

3. Click **Start scan**.

4. Look click though the list of detected files in turn, and look for any that the tool says should be removed (some files will be legitimate). Select the files to be removed ① and click the **Clean up checked items** button.

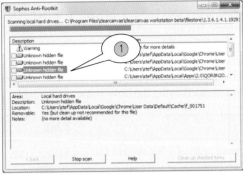

Check whether the file should be removed

The bottom window of the program will advise you on whether or not a file should be removed or not.

Discover Infections Hooked into the Windows Kernel with SanityCheck

The Kernel is the central component of your Windows system, and can be thought of as Windows' central nervous system. The kernel is ultimately responsible for mediating all requests between your PC's software, including Windows, and the hardware devices that constitute your PC, such as the RAM, processor and graphics card. It is the first process that Windows loads when it starts up, and if it fails then your PC will crash.

Kernel hooks are a mechanism whereby legitimate programs can attach themselves to the running Kernel and perform low-level tasks, such as intercepting legitimate calls to kernel functions by normal applications and replacing the kernel function with their own. Due to improved alternative kernel interfaces in newer versions of Windows kernel hooks are now very rarely used by programmers, but they are still present in the running kernel. Unfortunately, kernel hooks can be exploited by rootkit writers to hide the software they inject into your PC.

SanityCheck is a free tool to analyse your running kernel and check if any programs are making use of kernel hooks. Before you run SanityCheck, you need to first disable your anti-virus, anti-spyware and firewall programs. This is because these types of security program make use of kernel hooks and so will create erroneous results. To run SanityCheck, follow these steps:

1. Start the SanityCheck program.

2. Click on the **Analyse** button. Any programs using Kernel hooks will be highlighted in red.

3. Once the analysis has completed, scroll down to the **Analysis** ② section to find any potential problems, and then to the **Conclusions** section to see what you should do next.

If you're unsure what any of the results mean, try searching the Web for the relevant kernel hook and program names to see if they belong to known infections.

Check the Analysis section for problems

 Click **Expert Mode** to see more details on the list of processes and kernel hooks.

Remove Unwanted Rootkits in XP with RootkitRevealer

RootkitRevealer provides excellent protection from rootkits on XP systems by scanning your system at two different levels. It performs a high-level scan, looking through the Windows software libraries for the files that are reported as being on the hard drive. It then performs a low-level scan of the hard drive and compares the files it finds to what is reported by Windows. Discrepancies mean that a rootkit is installed and interfering with the operation of the Windows software libraries.

By performing two scans, RootkitRevealer is not just relying on the Windows software libraries which may be infected, making it extremely difficult for a rootkit to hide itself.

To run RootkitRevealer, make sure that you are using an Administrator account, and that no other software is running, then follow the steps below:

1. Open the RootkitRevealer program.

2. Confirm that you accept the software terms.

3. Click on the **Scan** button ③. Any discrepancies found during the scan will be displayed ④.

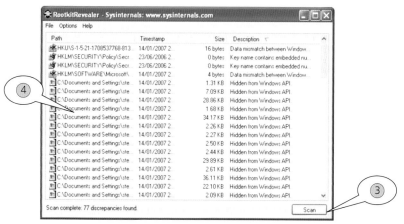

Using RootkitRevealer on Windows XP

If you find that discrepancies are reported, they could either be due to rootkits or false positives. To check on whether the discrepancies found on your system are serious or not, check out the listing of RootkitRevealer false positives on the RootkitRevealer forum:

http://forum.sysinternals.com/

If you can't find your specific files listed, post a question to the forum asking if anyone else has had similar results. To remove the infection, try one of the rootkit tools mentioned in this chapter, or search for specific removal instructions on the Web.

Keep Your PC 'Rootkit Resilient' with these Easy Prevention Tips

Although rootkits can be very difficult to get rid of once you are infected, there are a number of things you can do to make sure your PC is as protected as possible from the rootkit threat. Firstly, never run software that someone has emailed to you or you have found on the web unless you are 100% sure it is safe. Never, ever install software advertised to you through a Web pop-up window claiming to have detected problems on your PC.

Always keep your PC up-to-date with the latest Microsoft patches. Rootkits, like all malicious software, tend to exploit weaknesses in Windows that are periodically discovered, before they are patched by Microsoft. It is essential to always apply the latest patches to minimise the risk. Make sure that your PC is set to install updates automatically by following the steps given in Chapter 1.

Give your PC thorough virus and spyware scans regularly, and use the rootkit checking tools covered in this chapter to check for potential infections, removing any that are found.

Checklist: Minimise the Risk of Rootkit Infections

✓ Rootkit infections are designed to hide deep inside your PC, so are difficult to detect.

✓ Your normal anti-virus software will probably not detect a rootkit, so you need to use specialised scanning tools.

✓ Keeping your PC up-to-date will minimise the likelihood of rootkit infection.

✓ A virus scanner will block the Trojan infections that deliver rootkits to your PC.

✓ Giving your PC a regular scan with rootkit detection software will ensure that you remain rootkit free.

7: Lock Down the Security of Internet Explorer with Advanced Registry Tweaks

Tweaking the registry will give you complete control over many aspects of your PC's security, including many settings that cannot be configured anywhere else in Windows. However, before you start making any changes in the registry, you should create a complete registry backup, in case you need to undo any of the changes made.

To backup the registry in Windows 7 and Vista, set a Manual System Restore Point by following the steps given on page 55. XP users should follow the steps on page 56.

Prevent Internet Explorer from Caching Passwords

Allowing Internet Explorer to save your usernames and passwords makes it quick and easy to sign in to secure sites, but it also means that anyone else who uses your computer – or potentially a hacker who gains access to your machine – can obtain your login credentials. With a quick tweak of the registry you can turn off the password caching feature of Internet Explorer, removing the possibility that you accidentally store a sensitive password and increasing your PCs security in turn.

To apply this tip, follow the steps below:

1. Press **[Windows Key]** + **[R]**, type **REGEDIT** and click **OK**.

2. Navigate to the registry key: **HKEY_CURRENT_USER\Software\ Microsoft\Windows\CurrentVersion\Internet Settings**.

3. Check in the right-hand panel for the **DisablePasswordCaching** setting. If it doesn't exist, create it by right-clicking on a blank area of the right-hand panel and choosing **New > DWORD Value**.

4. Double-click on **DisablePasswordCaching**.

5. Change the Value data field to **1** and click **OK**.

You need to close the Registry Editor and restart Windows for the changes to take effect.

Prevent Applications from Changing Your Home Page

Certain disreputable programs, when installed, will try to modify your Internet Explorer home page so that you see an advertisement for their product or company. If you share you PC with other family members you may also find that they periodically reset your home page to some site of their choosing, either accidentally or on purpose. You may also find that a virus or spyware infection on your PC modifies your home page setting – however it happens, finding that your home page has changed can be very annoying.

However, by limiting the user accounts that can change the Internet Explorer settings in your registry, you can limit the possibilities for the home page to be changed. Here's how to do it:

1. Press [**Windows Key**] + [**R**], type **REGEDIT** and click **OK**.

2. Navigate to the registry key: **HKEY_CURRENT_USER\Software\ Microsoft\Internet Explorer\Main**.

3. Right-click on **Main** and select **Permissions**.

4. Click on the **Advanced** ① button.

5. Select your username and click **Edit**.

6. Tick the **Deny** option for **Set Value**.

7. Click **OK > OK > OK**.

8. Close the Registry Editor.

If you find that Windows occasionally throws up an error message when you try to alter any setting (not just Internet related) it can indicate a problem with registry permissions. Try carrying out the above steps for the registry key you are having problems with, but untick the **Deny** option in step 6.

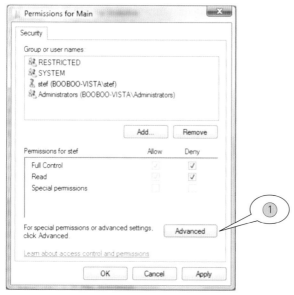

Control the security settings of individual registry keys

After applying the fix, you will find that many of your Internet Explorer settings can't be changed – this is what we wanted to happen, since it will prevent other users and applications from making unauthorised changes.

> If you yourself need to alter a setting, repeat the steps above and untick the **Deny** option in step 6. Remember: once you've made the change you need, lock the settings again.

Prevent Websites from Installing Software on Your PC

Some websites try to fool you into installing software on your PC, usually through some JavaScript code that tries to force the download on to your machine. With a quick tweak of the registry you can configure Internet Explorer to block downloads from certain websites, while still being able to visit those sites. Use this tip when there is a site you need to visit, but you don't want all of the malware and scareware software that it might try to install.

Here's how to secure Internet Explorer against unwanted downloads:

1. Press [**Windows Key**] + [**R**], type **REGEDIT** and click **OK**.

2. Navigate to the registry key: **HKEY_LOCAL_MACHINE\SOFTWARE\ Microsoft\Windows\CurrentVersion\Internet Settings\ZoneMap\ Domains**. If the Domains key doesn't exist, create it by right-clicking **ZoneMap** and selecting the **New > Key** option.

3. Right-click on **Domains** and choose **New > Key**.

4. Name the new key after the domain name of the site you want to block. For example, to block downloads from www.domain.com you would create a key named **domain.com**.

5. Click on the registry subkey that you just created, then right-click in a blank area of the right-hand panel and choose **New > DWORD Value**.

6. Name the new DWORD Value *.

7. Double-click on * and change the Value data field to **4**, then click **OK**.

8. Close the Registry Editor and restart your PC for the changes to take effect.

Prevent Users from Opening Files in Internet Explorer

There is a lot of crossover in the code Microsoft have used to implement Windows Explorer and Internet Explorer, meaning that many of the functions of Windows Explorer are also present in Internet Explorer. For example, you can use Internet Explorer to not only view web pages, you can also use it to view the files and folders installed on your PC. However, allowing web pages to link to your PC's files can prove to be a security risk, especially if you have applied group policy settings to prevent users from accessing Windows Explorer.

To prevent web pages from being able to link to local files, you should apply the following registry tweak:

1. Press [**Windows Key**] + [**R**], type **REGEDIT** and click **OK**.

2. Navigate to the registry key: **HKEY_LOCAL_MACHINE\Software\ Microsoft\Windows\CurrentVersion\Policies\Explorer**.

3. Right-click on a blank area of the right-hand panel and choose **New > DWORD Value**.

4. Name the new DWORD Value **NoFileUrl**.

5. Double-click on **NoFileUrl** and change the Value data field to **1**. Click **OK**.

6. Close the Registry Editor and restart your PC for the changes to take effect.

Block Users from Changing Internet Explorer Security Settings

The majority of Internet Explorer settings can be configured in the Internet Options control panel. However, once you've got Internet Explorer configured exactly how you want it for a combination of ease-of-use and security, it makes sense to block access to the Internet Options control panel, in order to prevent other users of your PC from making changes to your Internet Explorer settings that could potentially put your PC at risk.

By applying tweaks to the Internet Options control panel registry settings you can disable the different tabs of the control panel. To do so:

1. Press [**Windows Key**] + [**R**], type **REGEDIT** and click **OK**.

2. Navigate to the registry key: **HKEY_LOCAL_MACHINE\Software\ Policies\Microsoft\Internet Explorer\Control Panel**. If the Internet Explorer or Control Panel keys don't exist, create them by right-clicking on the previous key and selecting the **New > Key** option.

3. Right-click in a blank area of the right-hand panel and choose **New > DWORD Value**.

4. Refer to the table on the next page to find the first Internet Options function that you'd like to disable and name the DWORD Value, as appropriate.

5. Double-click on your new DWORD Value and change the Value data field to **1**. Click **OK**.

6. Repeat steps 4 and 5 for each function that you'd like to disable.

7. When finished, close the Registry Editor and re-boot your PC for the changes to take effect.

DWORD Value	Function
Accessibility	Disables all options under Accessibility
AdvancedTab	Removes access to the Advanced tab
CertifPers	Prevents changes to the Personal Certificate options
CertifPub	Prevents changes to the Publisher Certificate options
CertifSite	Prevents changes to the Site Certificate options
ConnectionsTab	Removes access to the Connections tab
ContentTab	Removes access to the Content tab
FormSuggest	Disables the AutoComplete for forms
GeneralTab	Removes access to the General tab
PrivacyTab	Removes access to the Privacy tab
ProgramsTab	Removes access to the Programs tab
ResetWebSettings	Disables the Reset Web Setting button
SecAddSites	Prevents adding new sites to any zone
SecChangeSettings	Prevents changes to the Security Levels for the Internet Zone
SecurityTab	Removes access to the Security tab
Settings	Blocks any changes to Temporary Internet Files

 You can re-enable an Internet Options control panel function by repeating the above steps and changing the Value data field to **0**.

Block ActiveX Controls from Being Installed

ActiveX controls allow extra functionality to extend Internet Explorer through add-ons downloaded from the Internet. Unfortunately, ActiveX controls are often used by hackers and virus writers to install their malicious software on your PC. With the application of a simple registry tweak, you can prevent Windows from installing ActiveX controls on your system, thus boosting your PC's security.

To apply the tweak, follow these steps:

1. Press **[Windows Key]** + **[R]**, type **REGEDIT** and click **OK**.

2. Navigate to the registry key: **HKEY_CURRENT_USER\Software\ Microsoft\Windows\CurrentVersion\Internet Settings\Zones\3** ②.

3. Right-click on a blank area of the right-hand panel and choose **New > DWORD Value**.

4. Name the new DWORD Value **1001** ③.

5. Double-click **1001** and set the Value data field to **3**. Click **OK**.

6. Close the Registry Editor and restart your PC for the changes to take effect.

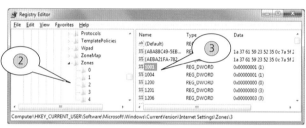

Edit the Internet Zone registry key

Strengthen Your IE Security Settings to Minimise the Risk of Hacker Attack

The Security Zones feature of the Internet Options control panel allows you to configure different security settings for different areas of the Internet. The control panel provides access to four different zones: Internet Zone, Local Intranet Zone, Trusted Sites Zone and Restricted Sites Zone. Applying settings to these different zones will allow you to control what the different websites contained in those zones can do on your PC.

However, Internet Explorer has a fifth security zone – the Local Machine Zone – which isn't listed in the Internet Options dialogue. The Local Machine Zone controls what Internet Explorer can do on your local computer, and the only way to configure it is via the registry.

The Local Machine Zone controls Internet content that is cached on your local computer. A hacker might try to push their malicious content into the local Internet cache, and then use that malicious content to install a virus on your PC. By configuring the Local Machine Zone in the registry you can prevent this from happening. Here's how:

1. Press [**Windows Key**] + [**R**], type **REGEDIT** and click **OK**.

2. Navigate to the registry key: **HKEY_LOCAL_MACHINE\Software\ Microsoft\Windows\CurrentVersion\Internet Settings\Zones\0**.

3. If the registry value 1200 doesn't exist, right-click in a blank area of the right-hand panel and choose **New > DWORD Value**. Name the new DWORD Value **1200**.

4. Double-click on **1200**, set the Value data field to **3** and click **OK**. This will prevent ActiveX controls being run from the local machine.

5. If the registry value 1201 doesn't exist, right-click in a blank area of the right-hand panel and choose **New > DWORD Value**. Name the new DWORD Value **1201**.

6. Double-click on **1201**, set the Value data field to **3** and click **OK**. This will prevent scripts that control ActiveX controls from being run from the local machine.

7. If the registry value 1400 doesn't exist, right-click in a blank area of the right-hand panel and choose **New > DWORD Value**. Name the new DWORD Value **1400**.

8. Double-click on **1400**, set the Value data field to **3** and click **OK**. This will prevent Active Scripting being run from the local machine.

9. If the registry value 1406 doesn't exist, right-click in a blank area of the right-hand panel and choose **New > DWORD Value**. Name the new DWORD Value **1406**.

10. Double-click on **1406**, set the Value data field to **3** and click **OK**. This will prevent access to data sources across domains.

11. If the registry value 1C00 doesn't exist, right-click in a blank area of the right-hand panel and choose **New > Binary Value**. Name the new Binary Value **1C00**.

12. Double-click on **1C00**, set the Value data field to **00 00 00 00** and click **OK**. This will prevent Java from being run from the local machine.

13. Close the Registry Editor and restart your PC for the changes to take effect.

Checklist: Ultimate Internet Explorer Protection via the Registry

✓ Some security settings can only be applied to Internet Explorer via the registry.

✓ Before editing the registry, always make sure you have an up-to-date backup.

✓ Strengthening your Internet Explorer security settings will minimise the risk of hacker attack.

✓ Locking down the control panel settings will prevent other users from making your PC insecure.

✓ Limiting what users can do in Internet Explorer will minimise the risk of malicious software being installed by accident.

100% Windows – 0% Stress!

In Just 3 Steps: Make Your Windows Fast, Safe and Error-free!

Almost everybody these days uses Windows. What few people realise, is how easy it can be to make your Windows work faster, better, and never crash again. The Windows Advisor is there for you 24 hours a day to help you maximise your Windows capacity and solve any problems you may have. We'll show you how to clear your computer of built-up errors, make it run at 'super-fast' speed, fix serious system crashes, protect your PC from the latest security threats, solve printer problems and much more...

The 458 page manual will show you how to effortlessly tune up your Windows, turn your PC into a security fortress, and make your computer crash-proof and error-free in just a few simple steps. Plus during your 6 week free trial you'll also have access to:

✔ **Thousands of Articles and Software in the Member's-only Area of the website**

✔ **Free Windows Technical Support during your 6 week Free Trial**

And as a thank you gift for trying the Windows Advisor we'll also give you a free DVD containing over 160 free tools.

Take advantage of this unique opportunity: Claim your free, no-obligation 6-week trial and get your free trial copy of The Windows Advisor and your Free DVD right now:

www.windowsadvisor.co.uk